AN INTRODUCTION TO ARAB POETICS

AN INTRODUCTION TO ARAB POETICS

Adonis

Translated from the Arabic
by Catherine Cobham

University of Texas Press, Austin

International Standard Book Number 0-292-73859-5 (cloth);
0-292-73860-9 (paperback)
Library of Congress Catalog Card Number 90-70476

First published as
Introduction à la poétique arabe
by Sindbad, Paris 1985

First University of Texas Press Edition, 1990

Typeset by AKM Associates (UK) Ltd, Southall, London
Printed in Great Britain

Contents

Preface

I first became interested in the theoretical aspects of writing poetry in the 1950s, the decade which saw the founding of the periodical *Shi^{c}r* (Poetry) in 1957 in Beirut. It soon became obvious to me that the prevailing critical outlook, especially in the universities and other educational establishments of the Arab world, was the product of a functionalist view of poetry. As a result, poetry had a semi-organic relationship with the establishment and its religious and social values. This was an approach which examined poetry — by its nature, concerned with the innermost depths of things — from the outside, except that paradoxically it was concerned more with the content of the verse than its manner of expression; in addition, this approach imprisoned Arabic poetry within an excessively rigid framework, so that it appeared to have nothing in common with any other poetry.

At the same period I decided to read the actual texts of Arabic poetry without reference to what the critics, ancient or modern, had written about them — something which took me about ten years. It became clear to me then that the prevailing interpretations of poetry were completely dependent on the power structure, which in turn was bound up with the religious establishment. In the texts themselves, however, there is scope for a pluralism of interpretation, confirming that Arabic poetry is not the monolith this dominant critical view suggests, but is pluralistic, sometimes to the point of self-contradiction. It is hard to imagine a more superficial, trivializing view of poetry, and one less conducive to an understanding of the poetic experience, than that which has long prevailed in the Arab world.

My reading also made it clear to me that, apart from the disparities resulting from linguistic and social peculiarities or from chronological differences, the artistic and cultural problems posed by writing poetry in Arabic are the same as those encountered in other societies.

Eventually I felt compelled to try to present Arabic poetry from another perspective, one which I have set out at length in the introductions to the three parts of *Dīwān al-Shi^{c}r al-^{c}Arabī* (Anthology of Arabic Poetry), and also in *Muqaddima li'l-Shi^{c}r al-^{c}Arabī* (An Introduction to Arabic Poetry).

I had become still more certain of the view of Arabic poetry which I was attempting to formulate when, at the beginning of the 1970s, I embarked upon a study of Arab culture as a whole which I called *al-Thābit wa'l-Mutaḥawwil: baḥth fi'l-ittibā^{c} wa'l-ibdā^{c} ^{c}inda'l-^{c}arab* (The Fixed and the Changing: A study of conformity and originality in Arab culture). This was published in three parts (with a fourth part in preparation), with the following subsidiary titles: *al-Uṣūl* (The Roots), *Ta'ṣīl al-Uṣūl* (Establishing the Roots) and *Ṣadmat al-Ḥadātha* (The Shock of Modernity).

The lectures I delivered at the Collège de France in 1984 (and which are published in the present volume) are thus the product of over a quarter of a century's research into Arabic poetry and Arab culture.

I hope they may serve as a preface to the writing of a new history of Arabic poetry based on the language of poetry itself in its relationship with things, and in its movement and depth of perspective. At the same time, I hope that they will open another window for English poetry, on to the language and particular creative vision of Arabic poetry.

Paris, January 1990

1
Poetics and Orality in the *Jāhiliyya*

I use the term orality here in three senses: first, to mean that Arabic poetry at the time of the *Jāhiliyya* (the pre-Islamic era in Arabia) was rooted in the oral and developed within an audio-vocal culture; second, to indicate that this poetry did not come down to us in written form but was 'anthologized' in the memory and preserved through oral transmission; and finally, to investigate the characteristics of this orality in poetry and assess the extent of its influence on written Arabic poetry in succeeding periods, in particular on its aesthetics.

Pre-Islamic poetry was born as song; it developed as something heard and not read, sung and not written. The voice in this poetry was the breath of life — 'body music'. It was both speech and something which went beyond speech. It conveyed speech and also that which written speech in particular is incapable of conveying. This is an indication of the richness and complexity of the relationship between the voice and speech, and between the poet and his voice; it is the relationship between the individuality of the poet and the physical actuality of the voice, both of which are hard to define. When we hear speech in the form of a song, we do not hear the individual words but the being uttering them: we hear what goes beyond the body towards the expanses of the soul. The signifier is no longer an isolated word, but a word bound to a voice, a music-word, a song-word. It is not merely an indication of a certain meaning, but an energy replete with signs, the self transformed into speech-song, life in the form of language. From this comes the profound congruence between the vocal and acoustic values of speech and the emotional and affective content of pre-Islamic poetry.

To start with, orality implies listening, for the voice appeals to the ear first of all. Orality therefore had its own art of poetic expression which lay not in what was said, but in how it was said. This was particularly important because, on the whole, the pre-Islamic poet spoke of what his listeners already knew: their customs and traditions, wars and heroic exploits, victories and defeats. Thus the poet's individuality manifested itself in his manner of expression: the more inventive this was, the more he was admired for his originality. It was his duty to give to the collective, to the everyday moral and ethical existence of the group, a unique image of itself in a unique poetic language. In doing this, the poet was not expressing himself as much as he was expressing the group, or rather he expressed himself only through expressing the group. He was their singing witness, and therefore we should not be surprised at this paradox in pre-Islamic poetry: unity of content and diversity of expression.

Let us say that recitation and memory did the work of a book in the dissemination and preservation of pre-Islamic poetry.

If we go back to the root of the word 'song' (*nashīd*) in Arabic, we see that it means the voice, the raising of the voice and the recited poetry itself. Two basic principles of pre-Islamic poetry were that it should be recited aloud and that the poet himself should recite his own poem: as al-Jāḥiẓ (775–868) says, a poem sounds better from the mouth of its composer. The Arabs of the pre-Islamic period considered the recitation of poetry as a talent in itself, distinct from that of composition; obviously it was of considerable importance in drawing an audience and impressing them enough to hold them there — especially so since, at the time, listening was essential to the comprehension of words and to musical ecstasy (*ṭarab*). For, in the words of Ibn Khaldūn (1332–1406), 'Hearing is father to the linguistic faculties.' From this perspective, the better the recitation, the more profound the effect of the poetry.

Recitation of poetry is a form of song. The Arab literary tradition is full of signs confirming this. The poets who recite their work are often compared to singing birds and their verses to birdsong. 'Song is the leading-rein of poetry,' according to a well-known expression, while Ḥasan Ibn Thābit (d. 674), 'the poet of the Prophet', has an equally famous verse:

> Sing in every poem you compose
> That song is poetry's domain.

Examples like these show the organic link that existed between poetry and song in the pre-Islamic period. This explains the significance of the claim that the Arabs 'measure poetry by song' or that 'Song is the measure for poetry.'[1] The critic Ibn Rashīq maintains that song was at the origin of rhyme and metre,[2] and that 'Metres are the foundations of melodies, and poems set the standards for stringed instruments.'[3]

Kitāb al-Aghānī (The Book of Songs) by Abu'l-Faraj al-Iṣfahānī (897–967), which consists of twenty-one volumes and took fifty years to compile, is the most striking proof that poetry in the pre-Islamic period was synonymous with recitation and song.

Ibn Khaldūn writes:

> In the early period singing was a part of the art of literature, because it depended on poetry, being the setting of poetry to

> music. The literary and intellectual elite of the Abbasid state occupied themselves with it, intent on acquiring a knowledge of the styles and genres of poetry.[4]

Elsewhere he defines the craft of song as 'the setting of poems to music by dividing the sounds into regular intervals'.[5]

The actual performance of poetry had its own rules in the pre-Islamic period which survived into later ages. Some poets, for example, recited standing up, while others proudly refused to recite unless they were seated. Some would gesture using their hands or their whole bodies, like the poetess al-Khansā' (sixth–seventh century) who, it is said, rocked and swayed, and looked down at herself in a trance. Thus in orality there is a 'meeting in action' of voice, body, word and gesture.

Some poets dressed up to perform, as if the occasion were a celebration like a wedding or a feast. In later times poets would imitate the costumes of their pre-Islamic forbears and so affirm the unbroken link between past and present.

Among the poets known for the excellence of their recitation in the pre-Islamic period was al-A^{c}shā (A^{c}shā Qays, d. 629), later given the nickname 'Cymbal of the Arabs' by the caliph Mu^{c}āwiya. There arc many different explanations of this name: it was said that the musical quality of the poet's performance transported his audience; that he sang out his poetry like a hymn of praise; that his contemporaries frequently sang his poetry; or simply that the name reflected 'the excellence of his poetry' or 'the beauty of his performance'. All of them link the poetry to vocal performance and song, the same connection made by Farazdaq (641–732), who declared to the poet ^{c}Abbād al-^{c}Anbarī (seventh–eighth century) after hearing him recite, 'Your recitation makes me better able to understand the beauty of the poetry.'[6]

Song was a body whose joints were metre, rhythm and melody.

The aural response depended on how well these parts worked together in performance — song was a discipline of the voice which required a corresponding aural discipline. The need to co-ordinate the various elements of song led gradually to the devising of special rhythmic structures.

Most scholars would agree that rhythm began in the pre-Islamic period with *saj*^{c} (rhymed prose or rhyme without metre). *Saj*^{c} was the first form of poetic orality, that is poetic speech following a single pattern. This was followed by *rajaz*, a type of metre made up of either a single hemistich like *saj*^{c}, but divided into regular rhythmic units, or of two hemistichs. The *qaṣīd* (ode, poem) was the culmination of this development of rhythmic forms, and consisted of two rhythmically balanced hemistichs which took the place of the balancing assonances of *saj*^{c} and *rajaz*.

The root of the word *saj*^{c} contains a reference to song, and is used to denote both the musical call of the pigeon and the plaintive monotonous cry of the she-camel, alike in the one respect of being continuous, unvarying sounds. Hence *saj*^{c} came to mean 'proceeding in an even, uniform way' and was adopted as a technical term to describe a form of rhythmic speech with end rhymes, like poetry, but no metre, and a quality of evenness and regularity and sameness in speech, such that every word in a sentence resembles the other.[7]

Technically there are three types of *saj*^{c}:

1. In the same statement, the different parts balance one another and are of equal length, and the assonances are identical and fall at the same point in each part.

2. The statement is composed of two parts, and each word in the first part is assonant with the word corresponding to it in the second part. According to rhetoricians this is the most pleasing form of *saj*^{c} as long as it is not forced or overdone.

3. The parts are equal and the assonance is to be found in sounds which are close, but not identical.

In the early years of Islam the use of *saj^c* declined until the form had almost disappeared, perhaps because of its association with soothsaying in the pre-Islamic period. According to a *ḥadīth* (saying of the Prophet), Muhammad declared, 'Beware of the *saj^c* of the soothsayers,' and he is said to have banned its use in prayer and discourse. However, it reappeared in later times and was used especially in literary prose such as sermons, epistles and *maqāmāt*, eventually with so much exaggeration and artificiality that it became no more than an empty mould.

The poem (*qaṣīd*) is composed of verses divided into two equal halves or two hemistichs. It is said that the root (*qaṣada*) here means to break in half and so the term *qaṣīd* refers to the actual shape of the poem which is in two columns. However Ibn Khaldūn believes that the term derives from the way the poet keeps starting new subjects, passing 'from one sort of poetry to another, and from one subject (*maqṣūd*) to another, tempering the first subject and the ideas connected with it until it fits harmoniously with the next'.[8] In an alternative explanation al-Jāḥiẓ writes that the *qaṣīd* was so named 'because the composer [of the poem] creates it in his mind and has an aim for it (*qaṣada lahu qaṣdan*) . . . and strives to improve it. [The word *qaṣīd*] is formed on the pattern *fa^{c}īl*.'[9]

The *qaṣīd* form was predominant perhaps because it was the best able to respond to the 'needs of the soul' as al-Jāḥiẓ puts it, and the most susceptible to being sung and recited.

The fact that each verse (*bayt*) in the *qaṣīd* is an independent unit relates to the demands of recitation and song and their effect on the listener and not, as some people believe, to the nature of the Arab mind which they claim is preoccupied with the parts at the expense of the whole.

It should also be stressed that the rhyme in the *qaṣīd* relates first and foremost to its musical performance. One of the conditions for its use was that it should not be there for its own sake but as an integral part of the texture of the verse, in harmony with the metre and sense and in no way an extraneous addition or superfluous padding. The rules concerning 'the end of the verse', the rhyme which had to be repeated at the end of each line throughout the poem, applied to both vowels and consonants: the 'i' vowel (*kasra*) and the 'u' vowel (*ḍamma*) were not supposed to be interchanged, for example; the same rhyme word was not to be repeated in the course of a poem, and each verse had to be independent in sense from the following one. All these conditions support the idea that rhyme was present basically for its musical qualities, that is for the vocal-rhythmic phrasing, and was not a mere grouping of vowels and consonants. It was therefore necessary for the repeated consonants to resemble one another, and for particular care to be taken with the final vowel sound because on it depended the quality of the psalmody. The rhyme gave to the verse and thence to the whole poem a harmony and symmetry which ensured that it possessed a spiritual, musical and temporal cohesiveness.

The characteristics of pre-Islamic poetic orality formed the basis for the major part of the criticism and theory of poetry in subsequent periods. Rules and criteria were evolved which still dominate not only the technique of poetry but the tastes, ideas and areas of knowledge reflected in it.

To study these questions exhaustively would require an entire history of Arab poetics, so I will restrict myself to discussing the three points which are the most relevant to my subject here: inflexion (*iʿrāb*), metre and the activity of listening.

It is important to note that the Arabs codified poetic orality, giving its conventions and practices systematic formulations, in the early years of the interaction between Arab-Islamic and other cultures, in particular Greek, Persian and Indian. The aim of this was to affirm, preserve and put into practice the rhetorical and musical specificity of the craft of Arabic poetry, thereby asserting its individual identity and that of the Arab poet. This eager pursuit of distinctiveness and specificity lay at the root of Arab intellectual activity during this period of social and cultural mingling between the Arabs and other peoples, especially in Basra (Iraq), the cultural capital, 'mediator to the earth and heart of the world', as an Arab historian has described it. Solecisms and mispronunciations had become widespread in the language. The Persians had introduced Persian words and some rules of grammar, as well as popularizing their music. Ṭaha Ḥusayn (1889–1973) characterizes the cultural situation at the time as a mixture of:

> pure Arab culture based on the Qur'ān and related religious sciences, and poetry and the lexical and grammatical issues which it raised; Greek culture based on medicine and philosophy; and an oriental culture stemming originally from the Persians, the Indians and the Semitic peoples in Iraq.[10]

In this climate the rules of language were laid down for fear that solecisms and corruptions would creep into the Qur'ān and the *ḥadīths*. Poetic metres were fixed to preserve the rhythms of poetry and to distinguish them from Greek, Syriac, Persian and Indian metres and rhythms, and rules for the composition, appreciation and transmission of poetry were laid down.

In the *Muqaddima* Ibn Khaldūn discusses the introduction of a system of rules into linguistic and poetic orality. He says that the Arabs recited and sang their poetry guided by their instincts and natural aptitude; they had no rules to bring order t relied instead on their taste and perceptions. As 'Hearing to the linguistic faculties,' according to Ibn Khaldūn, an linguistic aptitude of the Arabs changed 'with the variati s which they heard from non-Arab speakers of Arabic', Arab scholars feared that:

> this faculty would degenerate and as time went on the Qur'ān and the *ḥadīth* would no longer be understood. They therefore devised rules to govern this faculty, based on their normal way of speaking, which are now generally applicable, like universals and basic principles. They used them to classify all parts of speech by analogy, putting like with like. For example, the subject of the verb (*fā^{c}il*) takes the 'u' ending, the object (*maf^{c}ūl*) takes the 'a' ending and the subject of a nominal sentence takes the 'u' ending. Noting that with the change of vowels at the ends of words, a change in meaning occurs, they adopted the term *i^{c}rāb* (inflexion) for this change and *^{c}āmil* (agent) for that which necessitates the change. These terms and others like them which they coined became technical terms peculiar to them; they set them down in writing and developed them into a separate discipline, to which they gave the name *naḥw* (grammar).[11]

The first scholar to write on grammar was Abū'l-Aswad al-Du'alī (605–88). His work was revised and completed by al-Khalīl Ibn Aḥmad al-Farāhīdī (seventh century), who also wrote another work on language to preserve the conventional usages, fearing that they would become extinct and 'ignorance of the Qur'ān and *ḥadīth* would result'. This was:

> *Kitāb al-^{c}Ayn*, on lexicography, in which he dealt with all possible combinations of the letters of the alphabet, that is, with

words composed of two, three, four and five radicals, the last being the longest possible combination in Arabic.[12]

Abū'l-Aswad al-Du'alī was the first to systematize the case endings in the Qur'ān. It is said that he sent for a scribe and gave him the following instructions:

> If you see me opening my mouth to say a letter, then make a dot above the letter, up in the air. If I close my mouth, put the dot on the line in front of the letter, and if I say the vowel 'i' put it under the letter. If I follow any of the aforementioned with a nasal sound, then put two dots instead of one.

The dots were the earliest indications of the case endings (*i*^{c}*rāb*) to guide people to the correct pronunciation and thence to the correct meaning of the Qur'ān.

The *i*^{c}*jām*, or differentiation of certain letters of the alphabet by the use of diacritical points, was fixed after the *i*^{c}*rāb* by Naṣr Ibn ^{c}Āṣim al-Laythī (seventh century). He arranged the letters of the alphabet in groups according to their shapes, and distinguished between the similar-looking ones by either one or two diacritical points, some underneath the letters and some above.

Thus the *i*^{c}*rāb* was designed to distinguish between the various parts of the sentence by use of the 'u' vowel, the 'a' vowel and the 'i' vowel, and the *i*^{c}*jām* to distinguish between the letters which looked alike.

In completing the work of al-Du'alī, al-Khalīl represented the *fatḥa* ('a' vowel) by a small slanting *alif* above the letter, the *ḍamma* ('u' vowel) by a small *wāw* also above the letter, and the *kasra* ('i' vowel) by a recurring *yā'*, which eventually lost one of its two parts, placed under the letter. He also fixed the writing of the *hamza* (glottal stop), *tashdīd* (doubling of a consonant) and *idghām* (contraction of one letter into another). He attached the *fatḥa*, *kasra* and *ḍamma* to the basic unvowelled forms of the words for the first time, to help with their pronunciation, and this was the starting-point of his concern with the musicality of words.

Al-Khalīl studied the derivations, morphology and vowelling of words, and the letters and their linguistic sounds, alone or in combinations, and all the problems connected with the etymology of words. He analysed a word in isolation to understand its general structure, and examined it in different syntactical contexts. He is considered one of the founders of the discipline of phonetics, the study of words as groups of sounds.[13] His musical sense helped him to define the points of articulation of letters and to differentiate between their sounds, and this led him to devise patterns for nouns and verbs, and establish poetic metres.

Al-Khalīl's invention and classification of poetic metres was a work of great creativity which demonstrated not only his genuine musical sense but also his remarkable powers of analysis. In *Kitāb al-Mūsīqā al-Kabīr* (The Great Book of Music) by al-Fārābī (872–950) we find confirmation of al-Khalīl's creative genius: al-Fārābī discusses the relationship between poetry and music, as perceived by al-Khalīl, in a precise theoretical manner which helps us better to understand al-Khalīl's work and his pioneering role.

Al-Fārābī considers poetry and music as belonging to the same genre: they are governed by composition, metre and the relationship between movements and pauses. However, an essential difference separates them: poetry is an arrangement of words according to their meanings, ordered in a rhythmic structure and taking the rules of grammar into account, while music attempts to adapt rhythmic speech to its measures, and transmits it as sounds in harmonious relationships both quantitatively and qualitatively, according to its own methods of composition.

Al-Fārābī goes on to say that as in general the craft of poetry and rhymed or metric prose existed before that of music, and as poetry was sung before its metres were formally defined, and musical instruments were invented after song, the relationship of music to poetry is not a simple relationship of music to words but a very specific one. When speech is used to communicate at a basic level it is assumed that the words need do no more than make the listener feel he has understood what is intended. In this situation the time taken to articulate the words is that of everyday speech. But when the words are spoken in different relationships to one another by lengthening the vowels, and varying the intonation and pitch, then listening becomes a pleasurable activity in itself, the listener's attention is thoroughly aroused and the words have more of an effect on him. Articulating the words in this special way requires the sensitivity and imaginative power to produce the type of measured rhythm which binds the parts of the word together, and stops it disintegrating as the vowelled consonants are lengthened or shortened or concealed for the sake of the melody. Because words combined with melody — that is, with poetic metres — are the subject of linguistics, it follows that the music made by different groups is distinguished and differentiated according to the difference between languages and pronunciations and the methods of setting words to music in each language. We can understand from this that al-Khalīl's chief motive for establishing poetic metres was to differentiate Arabic poetry and its music from those of other languages. Thus metre as defined by him is the equivalent of an instrument, a basic principle — a kind of answer to the Persian and Indian musical instruments which had begun to proliferate in Arab-Islamic society at the end of the eighth century. This distinction of his relies on the specific phonological system and syllabic structure of the Arabic language, which makes it suitable for poetic composition and gives it an affinity with music.

Al-Fārābī maintains that the music of poetical speech is absolutely natural and considered superior to all other music in its evocative powers and the effect it produces. Because it is so natural to man, the Arabs and the peoples of the East in general attach tremendous importance to it. It affords pleasure and repose, and gladdens the ear, enriches the imagination and nourishes the emotional and contemplative faculties. Because the perfect tunes are those created by the human voice, that is, by the song rising naturally from the vocal chords, of which poetry is in a sense the product, the union of poetry with music is altogether natural.

Al-Fārābī divides these tunes into three categories, according to the divisions of poetic speech. He calls the first *al-muqawwiya* (the strengthener), that which gives the soul strength and increases its strong emotions. The second he calls *al-mulayyina* (the assuager), that which imparts gentleness and softness, and the third *al-muᶜaddila* (the balancer), that which creates a balance in the soul between strength and gentleness, and in so doing brings it calm and stability.

> Because many moral stances and actions are the result of the emotions and of the visions conjured up by the imagination [writes al-Fārābī], these perfect tunes have a beneficial effect on attitudes and morals and encourage the listeners to carry out the actions demanded of them and to acquire all the mental attributes such as wisdom and knowledge of the sciences.[14]

Al-Fārābī defines rhythm as 'a pattern which moulds the melody into time periods with specific intervals and of specific duration'.[15] The rhythms are classified according to time cycles called *uṣūl*, the smallest of which is binary.

The rhythmic units are the *sabab* (chord) and the *watid* (peg), and metre is merely a particular combination of these units, based on the following elements:

1. *Sabab* a. *khafīf* (light): a vowelled consonant followed by an unvowelled consonant;
   b. *thaqīl* (heavy): two consecutive vowelled consonants.
2. *Watid* a. *majmū*^{c} (assembled): two consecutive vowelled consonants followed by an unvowelled consonant;
   b. *mafrūq* (separated): two vowelled consonants separated by an unvowelled consonant;
   c. *maqrūn* (joined): a vowelled consonant followed by two unvowelled consonants.
3. A combination of *watid* and *sabab* — *taf*^{c}*īla*.
4. A combination of different parts of the hemistich.
5. The hemistichs (*miṣrā*': one half of a folding door, or *shaṭr*: a half).
6. The verse (*bayt*: tent, house).

It is clear from the above how metre can be viewed as an instrument or guiding principle; it is a particular rhythmic modality, that is a certain arrangement of the elements of a melody. According to al-Fārābī, the verse 'is only defined by the practice within each linguistic group'; in Arabic this is 'the utterance which is confined by one complete measure'.[16] Thus the verse, and this metric or melodic modality, are conventions of singing and recitation linked to pre-Islamic orality.

I now move on to the third issue, the relationship between poetic orality and the act of listening. Because of this relationship, poetry criticism revolved around the principle of listening and the link between the poetry and the audience. The poet of the *Jāhiliyya* did not create poetry for himself but for others, for those who listened to him in order to be moved by him. Poetic talent was judged by the poet's ability to invent something which would leave its mark on the listener's soul. The poet's basic preoccupation was therefore that his poem must correspond to what was in his listener's soul, because his eloquence was evaluated in terms of how much the listener understood of what he said. However, what was in the listener's soul was a part of the common code, and his comprehension merely reflected the prevailing common taste. So the merit of the poetry did not lie in what the poet affirmed, but rather in 'the manner of affirmation', as al-Jurjānī (d. 1078) puts it,[17] and the effect this had on the listener.

The poetry was therefore judged according to how far it could arouse *ṭarab*, a state of musical delight or ecstasy, and the poetics was founded on what could be called an aesthetics of listening and delight. This was then transformed by political exploitation and the general ideology into a sort of aesthetics of information, so that poetry became a variety of declamatory speech able to affect people in its own particular manner, through panegyric or satire, enticement or intimidation.

At the semantic level, this aesthetics of listening required the poet to avoid 'remote allusions, abstruse tales and ambiguous suggestions' and 'to aim at the opposite of these'.[18] It also required him 'to use metaphors which were close to reality, not remote from it',[19] because poetic speech should be 'based on what is useful, whether metaphoric or literal'.[20]

These beliefs regarding the nature of poetry were what brought about the separation of poetry from thought. Al-Jāḥiẓ goes so far as to assert that poetry is the antithesis of thought because, according to him, eloquence in poetry is that which can be understood without recourse to thought and requires no interpretation.[21]

This separation of poetry from thought reinforced the aesthetics of pre-Islamic orality as against an aesthetics of writing and confirmed a prejudice in favour of pure bedouinism as opposed to the ignoble ways of the town. It also implanted in people's minds a particular image of poetry as something to be recited aloud or sung. Perhaps this explains the importance attached by the critics to the concept of 'naturalness' (*badāha*) in poetry, a concept which was synonymous with spontaneity and instinct, and antithetical to refinement of technique (*taḥbīr*) and artificiality. Abū Sulayman al-Manṭiq (d. 985) defines *badāha* as 'a spiritual energy in a human temperament'.[22]

As regards form, this aesthetic demands expressions which are musical and agreeable, according to al-Fārābī, so that the art of poetry appears like 'the leader of the group of musicians'.[23] Al-Fārābī holds that a melody which is beautiful and a pleasure to listen to is one where beauty of sound is joined with words which are easily understood, and he lists the qualities which characterize the most beautiful poetic melodies:

1. purity: where there is nothing in the melody to spoil it quantitatively or qualitatively;
2. phrasing long passages by use of rocking and swinging rhythms to break them up;
3. suppleness and delicacy in long-drawn-out melodies;
4. controlling some parts of the melody by closing the lips so that the sound comes out through the nose;
5. giving melodies a nasal twang by allowing some of the sound to come out through the lips and some through the nose;
6. the use of swift jogging tunes;
7. strong accentuation of the melody in some parts;
8. some use of the chest for emphasis, especially in tunes intended for the male voice.

These characteristics can only spring from a diction which is easy, clear, supple and flexible, and abounds in vowelled letters. These letters harmonize and marry with melody and 'make a statement which does not disgust and impart a feeling which is not repugnant', as al-Fārābī expresses it. Because of these preferences, critics disliked the use of obscure phrases in poetry, and words made up of letters which were heavy and difficult to pronounce; they praised everyday expressions and words which were easy to pronounce and sounded agreeable, because such words made the meaning quickly accessible. Al-Jāḥiẓ summarizes the critics' standpoint on this question in the following way:

> The letters of the words and the verses of the poem should seem harmonious and smooth, supple and easy . . . gentle and pleasant, flexibly ordered, light on the tongue, so that the entire verse is like one word, and one word is a single letter.[24]

This is what is embodied in the following characterization of eloquence (*faṣāḥa*): 'The pure bedouin Arabs are the essence of perfect eloquence,'[25] and in the characterization of naturalness (*badāha*) as 'what differentiates the Arabs from other peoples in eloquent expression'.[26] It is the antithesis of an embellished style (*taḥbīr*), that is a style involving careful study and intellectual activity. *Taḥbīr* is an attribute of post-classical poetry and urban culture, the product of self-conscious technique, while *badāha* and natural aptitude are properties of bedouin poetry. These concepts led to a formulation of artistic standards in poetry, summed up by al-Jāḥiẓ as follows: 'The best kind of discourse is that whose meaning is present in the literal meaning of the words.'[27]

Various normative values resulted from these ideas, including the belief that different meanings require different metres, so that the poet should choose a metre appropriate to the meaning he wishes to express. This in turn led to the belief that there is a definite link between the nature of meanings and the nature of poetic rhythms. Serious or impassioned content requires long metres; subtle, gentle, jesting or dancing content requires short, light metres; and the names of the metres are derived from their characteristics, for example: *al-ṭawīl*, 'the long'; *al-khafīf*, 'the light'.

Rhyme, which always had to be present with metre in the contemporary definition of poetry, must have an agreeable ring and a sweet tunefulness. The poet must avoid any transgression against musicality, in particular rhyming with words which are composed of unmusical letters such as *thā'*, *khā'*, *shīn, ṣād, ḍād, ṭā'*, *dhā'*, *ghayn*, *dhāl*, *wāw*, *zay*. The beginning of the poem must be beautiful. If the beginning is ugly, the listener will be repelled. If beautiful, he will be drawn into it and delighted by it and listen with interest to what follows.

From the above it is clear that the view of poetry in Arab-Islamic society, particularly in the early years, was dictated by pre-Islamic orality. The poem was perceived as call and response, the dialectic of a mutual invitation between the poet and the group; it was as if the aim of the poet in composing his poem, and that of the group or tribe in listening to it, coincided by prior agreement. In this situation there was no difference between poetry and life: life was poetry and poetry life, and so the structure of the poem corresponded to the movement involved in the act of communication as well as to its effectiveness and its ultimate intention. Rhythm is the basis of pre-Islamic poetical speech because it is a living energy binding the self to the other. It is the pulse of the living being, bringing together the movements of body and soul.

Rhyme was the basic element which distinguished pre-Islamic Arabic poetry from the poetry of other peoples. Neither in Aramaic, Syriac, Hebrew or Greek was it considered an essential feature of poetry in the way it was for the Arabs. Because of this, the ancient Arab critics maintained that the structure of pre-Islamic prosody was not an imitation of that of any other nation but was exclusive to the Arabs. They considered that it had passed through several stages, beginning with the chant of the camel-driver to his beasts, made up of words and sounds which seemed to follow rhythmic patterns, and with the chants and cries of war, and culminating in the musical units called *tafāᶜīl*. Particular care was taken with rhyme because it was the repository of the meaning, and because it was the natural sound which took the place in the verse of the gesture accompanying the speaker's words.

Some scholars think that rhyme led the way to the discovery of metre. Rhyme is more ancient than metre; it was known in the different forms of *sajᶜ*. The poets of the *Jāhiliyya* understood instinctively that for the sake of the rhythm there had to be agreement between the spiritual movements of the meanings and the verbal movements of the metres, so that the former were moulds for the latter. If the meaning changed and the spiritual movements changed as a result, then the metre must change too.

This is why the pre-Islamic poem was like a song, with a unity between the movement of speech and that of the body. It was many-sided, a grouping and combining of independent units, not only at the level of each part of the poem, but at the level of each verse within each part. This also accounts for its rhythmical strength and clarity in musical terms, its effectiveness as a means of communication, and the frequency with which it was memorized and repeated.

These considerations have led some scholars to assert that metre in pre-Islamic poetic orality was not a rule imposed from without, to which poetic form had to submit, but that poetic form was in itself metre. Others have gone so far as to say that the encounter between poet and listener was not only an act of participation in life and in the emotions: it was also a collective festival.

I have discussed the theory of pre-Islamic poetic orality in a simplified and descriptive way. Whatever the critical discourse concerning it, pre-Islamic poetry is clearly our earliest poetry: here the foundations were laid for Arabic speech to confront life and for the Arab to confront himself and the other for the first time. It was not only a conscious application of speech, but also a conscious participation in the act of existence. Our awareness of history is expressed for the first time in this poetry, and a large part of the Arab group unconsciousness is stored there. When we read it today we are reminded of our earliest voice and we hear how the sounds of the language embraced history and mankind. It is the first artistic embodiment of the language which we use to express who we are and to open up pathways into the darkness of the unknown. As such it is not only our first memory but the first wellspring of our imagination.

Today, however, we are confronting a crisis in our relationship with this poetry, caused by the very interpretation and theorization of it which I have just discussed. This critical discourse, having defined the characteristics of pre-Islamic poetry as oral poetry, then transformed them into absolute criteria for written poetics: henceforth poetry was only to be considered as poetry if its metres followed the rules of oral poetry, as laid down by al-Khalīl. These rules prevailed, drawing the dividing line between poetry and non-poetry. The climate of rule-making and intellectualization, generated by the climate of ideological struggle between the Arabs and other peoples in the seventh to the tenth centuries, helped these rules to become firmly established. Thus, instead of metre being considered as a regulating device for reciting and singing in a particular type of speech, it came to be viewed as the essence of all poetical speech. As a result, the written poetic text was viewed by the critics as if it were an oral text, in so far as all that writing demands — contemplation, exploration, abstruseness, thought itself — was banished from the domain of poetry. In other words, although oral and written poetry involve two different physical activities, the same critical standards were applied to both. Thus the critical discourse which pre-Islamic poetry generated in the past, and continues to generate, is the very thing which obscures that poetry from us.

Al-Khalīl was a specialist in the fields of grammar, rhetoric and music. He viewed language as a structure, and studied the music of pre-Islamic poetry, establishing and codifying its metres within a frame of reference whose purpose was to affirm that the Arabs too had their own particular music, with features which were purely Arab, especially as regards recitation and song. In all of this he proceeded in a scholarly manner, describing his findings and constructing theories on the basis of his descriptions. His work was of historic importance for the preservation of the language and the poetical metres. It was on a par with the work done by other scholars to record and preserve the Qur'ān and the traditions of the Prophet and the various achievements of the Arabs.

However, al-Khalīl's successors read a nationalist ideology into his descriptive work and, influenced by the political, cultural and nationalist struggles between the Arabs and other peoples, raised it to the level of a set of normative rules. This was how poetical speech became confined by specific metrical systems rather than remaining free, its movement dependent on the creative power of the poet.

Today when we read the poets of the past it is not only to see what al-Khalīl and his successors saw, but also to see what was hidden from them, what they did not see. We read the blank spaces which they left. Legislation and codification go against the nature of poetic language, for this language, since it is man's expression of his explosive moods, his impetuousness, his difference, is incandescent, constantly renewing itself, heterogeneous, kinetic and explosive, always a disrupter of codes and systems. It is the search for the self, and the return to the self, but by means of a perpetual exodus away from the self.

In this reading, we must examine the silence and ask questions of it: why did a single critical and legislative discourse prevail which expressed a uniform point of view, despite the many different voices involved? Did it eclipse the others, and if so why, and how? Was it considered the only correct view of poetry, and how had this come about? How was it decided that pre-Islamic poetry could only be understood and evaluated according to this view, when reading it today we become aware of a diversity which demands a more pluralistic and complex critical response? Did more diverse views exist, and were they obscured or forbidden? Why? How? Was there an authority which monopolized this prescriptive discourse to the point where others ceased to exist? Was this authority religious, linguistic, nationalistic? Did it represent a commitment to bedouinism — symbol of purity and authenticity; and a rejection of the city — symbol of hybridization and a lowering of standards? Was it an amalgamation of all this? Is the continuation of this discourse, the repetition of these same views and axioms, an assertion of identity, and is this why it has a tendency to suppress all others which may cast doubt on it, so that identity becomes mere reiteration of the same thing?

These questions all imply that behind this permanent, uniform, prescriptive discourse there exists a silence, an absence, a blank. Today we are called upon to embark on a reading of our critical heritage which will reveal these absences and make the silence speak.

2
Poetics and the Influence of the Qur'ān

To summarize the discussion in the preceding lecture: the first scholar to treat the most important features of pre-Islamic orality — metre and rhyme — from a theoretical point of view was al-Khalīl Ibn Aḥmad al-Farāhīdī. He studied the music of pre-Islamic poetry with a view to establishing the distinguishing features of Arab poetry and music, at a time when there was much intermixing of the Arabs and other peoples and widespread interaction and conflict of cultural values. In such circumstances the sense of identity and of difference increased and one particular approach to pre-Islamic poetry took precedence. As a result, the criteria of poetic orality reigned supreme and congealed into a set of formulae and directives which turned poetry into a parody of itself and failed to distinguish between the nature of the oral and written texts. The main preoccupation of the critics who advocated these standards was to maintain and assert the outward signs of the continuation of the tradition of pre-Islamic poetry because it was, in their view, the clearest and most powerful embodiment of the Arab identity. They considered any deviation from this orality a betrayal of identity, a deviation from the Arab poetic ideal and a devaluation of the very idea of poetry. Thus they confined their interests to a pursuit of the forms which would ensure the perpetuation of orality, generalizing from their particular features and conferring an absolute character on them, as if they were mathematical postulates or religious precepts. It was as if Arabic poetry, according to them, had to be reflected for ever in the exemplary mirror of pre-Islamic poetry.

While al-Khalīl was the first theoretician of poetic orality from the point of view of rhythm, al-Jāḥiẓ led the way in the theoretical study of the particularities of its linguistic features and poetic approach. Al-Jāḥiẓ considers that Arabic is superior to all other languages and that the Arabs are the 'source of perfect eloquence'; eloquence does not lie merely in an ability to communicate, as communication can be achieved without it; rather it is communication practised by the most eloquent members of society, the implication being that eloquence is a characteristic of the manner of expression rather than the meaning. Since, as al-Jāḥiẓ sees it, meaning is common to all peoples, while the form of expression is restricted and particular, poetic quality must relate to expression, not to content. Therefore poetic value springs from what is restricted and particular: the language. The only way to understand the particular merit of any poetry is to identify the characteristics which make it different from other poetry — in the case of Arabic poetry, these are form and metre.

This point of view leads al-Jāḥiẓ to believe that poetry, like language, is for the Arabs an instinct, an innate quality, a remarkable trait of nature, as he puts it, which cannot be explained because it is God-given. This accounts for his definition of the approach taken by Arab poets to the world about them: 'For the Arabs everything is intuition, improvisation, as if they were inspired. There is no effort, no suffering, no long reflection . . . as is the case with the Persians, Indians and Greeks.' It also explains his attitude to the translation of Arabic poetry. He writes, 'Arabic poetry is untranslatable and cannot be adapted to another language. When this is attempted, its structure is shattered, its metre is destroyed, its beauty disappears and its marvels fall away.' Thus the poetry 'collapses': everything that is special or distinctive about it ceases to exist and only the common and universal elements remain. Given these beliefs of his, we can understand why he claims that, 'The interest of Arabic poetry is confined to Arabs and those who speak Arabic fluently.'

The Qur'ān was not only a new way of seeing things and a new reading of mankind and the world, but also a new way of writing. As well as representing a break with the *Jāhiliyya* on an epistemological level, it represented a break on the level of forms of expression. The Quranic text was a radical and complete departure: it formed the basis of the switch from an oral to a written culture — from a culture of intuition and improvisation to one of study and contemplation, and from a point of view which made contact with the pagan surface of existence to one which reached into its metaphysical depths.

It is not my intention here to discuss the Quranic text from a religious or aesthetic point of view; there are many works which treat these subjects with perception and understanding. I shall confine myself to explaining the new horizons which the written structure of the Qur'ān opened up to Arab poetics.

I shall begin with a brief chronological review of studies that compare the Quranic text and poetical texts. It is true that they are mainly aimed at establishing how the two types of text differ, and confirming the superiority of the Qur'ān. At the same time, by the very act of comparison — and perhaps unintentionally — they convert the Qur'ān into a new literary ideal that transcends the old pre-Islamic ideal. This attracted the attention of poets and literary critics — especially those who had not taken orality as a model for poetry or an ideal of critical taste — and led them to look to the Qur'ān for guidance and inspiration.

One of the first studies to compare the Qur'ān and pre-Islamic poetry was *Majāz al-Qur'ān* (The Metaphor of the Qur'ān) by Abū ᶜUbayda (728–825). Written at the beginning of the ninth century, this work examines the metaphorical usage of language in the Qur'ān, paving the way for a critical approach which was to be concerned with the study of artistic imagery and of different means of expression.

Another early work was *Maᶜānī al-Qur'ān* (The Meanings of the Qur'ān) by al-Farrā' (d. 822), a study of the style of the Qur'ān from a structural and grammatical point of view. This takes the form of an exegesis of the Qur'ān, sura by sura; the author gives a grammatical, linguistic and literary commentary on each verse, sometimes supporting his interpretation with examples from pre-Islamic poetry. In the course of this exercise he talks of figurative devices such as metonymy, simile, allegory, metaphor, inversion, and the shifting of voice from the second person to the third. He discusses the musicality of the Qur'ān, which in his opinion stems from the arrangement of the words, the harmony of the sounds, and the agreement of rhymes at the ends of verses. He attempts to construct a theoretical view of this rhythmic phenomenon by comparing it to the metres of pre-Islamic orality, indicating, for example, the changes likely to affect words at the ends of verses in order to preserve musical harmony and create cadences, as with rhyme in poetry.

Al-Jāḥiẓ goes further than al-Farrā' in his attempts to discover the artistic mysteries of the Quranic text, in particular in his analysis of its metaphoric language and musicality of composition. He frequently supports his opinions with quotations from pre-Islamic poetry and writes at length on the metres of the Qur'ān, denying any similarity between them and the metres of poetry.

Towards the end of the ninth century, Ibn Qutayba (828–89) makes a perceptive analysis of rhetoric in the Quranic text in *Mushkil al-Qur'ān* (The Problematic of the Qur'ān). He defines its structure as a particular combination of words in perfect harmony with their meanings. Its musicality is produced by the internal rhythms of the verses based on the melodic agreement of individual sounds and the recurrence of the same end rhymes or variations of the end rhymes according to particular patterns. He discusses the effect which the Qur'ān has on the human soul, because it addresses it as one who knows its deepest secrets and therefore moves and captivates it. In his discussion of metaphor in the Qur'ān, Ibn Qutayba states that God made Arabic poetry occupy 'the position which books occupy in other cultures, and made it a repository for Arab sciences, and protected it with metres and rhymes and beauty of composition'. He observes that repetition in the Qur'ān is of great rhetorical value: it makes the text more emphatic and definite, filling out the meaning or extending the means of expression, depending on the context. He concludes by saying that the Qur'ān is in the mainstream of Arabic speech, but is superior to it, indeed incomparable.

Basing his argument on the text of the Qur'ān, al-Rummānī (908–94) offers a definition of rhetoric which differs from those that have gone before. In *al-Nukat fī I^{c}jāz al-Qur'ān* (Points Relating to the Inimitability of the Qur'ān), he states that rhetoric is not merely a question of making a meaning understood, but of 'imparting the meaning to the heart by the most beautiful form of expression'. In this definition he brings together the two extremes of rhetoric: its stylistic methods and the effects it creates. He studies rhetorical figures and the ways of using them, expressions and the techniques of composition, and end-rhymes which he defines as 'similar sounds in the pauses, which make sure that the meanings are well understood'. He concludes by establishing a sophisticated aesthetic criterion, claiming that the 'beautiful text' is 'the one which the spirit can approach in all manner of ways', or in modern critical terminology, the open text, the text with multiple meanings.

Bayān I^{c}jāz al-Qur'ān (An Explanation of the Inimitability of the Qur'ān) by al-Khaṭṭābī (d. 998) contains two features worthy of note: a more precise and comprehensive redefinition of Quranic composition than preceding ones, and an acknowledgement that culture is a prerequisite for artistic composition and for the understanding of art, confirming that spontaneity and fluency alone are not enough. This latter pronouncement perhaps represents the first glimmerings of a critique of pre-Islamic poetic orality and its aesthetic, albeit in an indirect fashion.

Al-Baqillānī (d. 1013), in his studies on the eloquence of the Qur'ān, refuses to make any comparisons between Quranic verses and verses of poetry or between suras of the Qur'ān and poems. This is because, in his opinion, the composition of the Qur'ān is a model of eloquence which does not resemble the artistic discourse of the Arabs in any of its forms, and is a complete departure from it. To make clear that such comparisons are inconceivable he classifies Arabic artistic speech under five headings:

1. poetry;
2. speech with a metre but no rhyme (*ghayru'l-muqaffā*);
3. rhymed speech (*saj^{c}*);
4. speech with a metre but no assonances (*ghayru'l-musajja^{c}*);
5. 'unrestrained' speech, that is, prose without rhyme or metre.

He concludes by claiming that the text of the Qur'ān falls into none of these categories, since its uniqueness makes it a special case. To clarify his point further, he analyses several Arabic texts, including sermons of the Prophet and his Companions and other celebrated Arab orators, the *Mu^{c}allaqa* of Imru'l-Qays (d. 540), representing 'ancient' poetry, and the poems of al-Buḥturī (820–97), representing 'modern'. He then points out the imperfections and failures of this poetry, compared with the Quranic text, and goes on to criticize those poets who harbour the illusion that they can profit from its example in their own poetical composition, and to praise those who continue to compose according to 'the Arab method', that is according to the traditions of pre-Islamic orality.

Studies devoted to language and poetry began to proliferate alongside these studies of the Quranic text. In the search for precision and accuracy, their authors draw comparisons between pre-Islamic poetry and the Qur'ān and discuss the problems of rhetoric common to both.[1] Manifest in these studies is the claim that no human being is capable of writing a text comparable to the Qur'ān. The suppressed antithesis is also present, however, expressed unambiguously by the Mu'tazilite al-Naẓẓām (d. 845): 'The composition of the Qur'ān is not a miracle. Human beings are capable of the same, and of better.'[2]

If we take these two elements together — the suppressed belief and the manifest assumption — we can better understand the extent to which the Qur'ān was the focal point of all the controversies relating to rhetoric and the aesthetics of speech in general, and to poetry and prose in particular; and moreover that it was a literary and artistic issue, as well as a religious-prophetic one. Thus we can say that the Qur'ān was read according to two different schemata. The first took as its reference point the rhetorical traditions of pre-Islamic poetry, relying on instinct and the values of the 'ancient' in its original form. The adherents of this way of reading studied the art of the Qur'ān (the 'heavenly text') guided by the standards of pre-Islamic poetry (the 'earthly text') and, conversely, studied the poetry in the light of the Qur'ān. Thus they bestowed upon pre-Islamic poetry the characteristics of a model or an ideal: 'The most beautiful form of human expression is pre-Islamic poetry, and in absolute terms the most beautiful form of expression, human or divine, using the very language of this poetry, is the Qur'ān.' This status made the poetry appear as an instinctive form of eloquence, also inimitable in its own way, which must serve as both source and model for later composition. Pre-Islamic poetic style was known as 'the Arab method', a term symbolizing the distinctive nature of Arab poetics.

Those who followed the second way of reading the Qur'ān attached importance not only to instinct but also to the culture which supported and nurtured this instinct. It was this reading which laid the foundations for what we may call 'the poetics of the written', which derived directly from oral poetics. These scholars considered the Qur'ān as a text of universal spiritual and intellectual dimensions; in their view, they were dealing not just with instinct, but with culture and a comprehensive spiritual and intellectual vision. If as a revealed text the language of the Qur'ān is divine or prophetic, it is at the same time poetic, using the very language of pre-Islamic poetry. And if it is sacred, being the language through which Islam was revealed, this sacredness is in some sense localized and historical. It conveys a vision both of the transcendental and of the human and cultural. It is the transcendental situated in time and space, or the transcendental and the immanent at the same time.

The import of this is that the Qur'ān in both of these readings is at the basis of the innovative cultural dynamism in Arab-Islamic society, its wellspring and its axis. It is the second reading, however, that paved the way for the transition from pre-Islamic poetic orality to a poetics of writing, whose principles were formulated in al-Jurjānī's theory of the composition of the Qur'ān. Several critics had already set this work in motion, notably al-Ṣūlī (d. 946). Thus we can say that the Qur'ān, which was regarded as constituting some sort of a rejection of poetry, led indirectly to the opening up of unlimited horizons in poetry and to the establishing of a genuine literary criticism.

Al-Ṣūlī offers the earliest near-complete defence of a poetics of writing, by which is meant here the 'modern method' represented by the poetry of Abū Tammām (788–845), as opposed to the 'method of the Arabs', the 'ancient method'. In defence of this modernity, which was at variance with the manner of the earlier poets — the poets of pre-Islamic orality — al-Ṣūlī emphasizes the following points:

1. The specific quality of the modern method lies in the invention both of meanings unknown to pre-Islamic orality and of a new poetic language. Modernization in poetry is therefore the invention of that which was unknown to the ancients.
2. The excellence of the poem itself must be the criterion by which it is judged, not its age. The best poetry is not necessarily the oldest. The method of the early poets is therefore not valid as a criterion.
3. A profound and comprehensive knowledge of culture is a prerequisite for anyone aspiring to be a critic of poetry; the critic must be 'one of those people who has an acute grasp of the science of poetry', as al-Ṣūlī puts it. The lack of this knowledge of culture in the critics of his time was what lay behind their ignorance of the specificity of the new poetry, including the poetry of Abū Tammām, and their hostility to the movement for poetic renewal, or to a poetics of writing.

Thus al-Ṣūlī asserts that Abū Tammām was the foremost exponent of the new style in poetry. In direct contrast to poetic orality, this new style was constructed around 'ambiguity and subtlety of meanings'. It was adopted by poets who 'favoured abstruse meanings, possessed [an elaborate] technique and were disposed to a subtle and philosophical manner of speech', in the words of al-Āmidī (d. 1155).

Al-Jurjānī brings to these issues, in particular to the poetics of writing, a coherent critical formulation in his two major works,

Asrār al-Balāgha (The Secrets of Rhetoric) and *Dalā'il al-I*^{c}*jāz* (Indications of Inimitability). He considers that composition (*naẓm*) is the essential element in revealing the poetical quality of a written text. This he defines as 'the attaching of words one to the other, making each one a reason for the other'.[3] By this he does not mean joining one thing to another haphazardly but arranging the words in accordance with the arrangement of the meanings in the soul, so that the meanings are harmonized and fit together as demanded by the intellect. Composition, according to this definition of his, is fine craftsmanship, resembling the silversmith's or goldsmith's art, and also that of the engraver, the colourist, the illuminator and all the arts which are concerned with representation.[4] This is reminiscent of al-Jāḥiẓ's definition of poetry as 'fine craftsmanship and a process of representation'.

Naturally then, in this theory of composition words are not to be looked at for their own sake, for a word:

> is not superior to another as a separate unit. Its merit and distinctiveness are confirmed only in the degree to which its meaning fits with the meanings which follow it. We often come across a word which delights us in one position and is irksome or strange in another.[5]

Similarly meanings are not considered for their own sake since they have no intrinsic worth in isolation. Meanings work in:

> the same way as colours from which paintings and illuminations are made up. The painter who can choose and manipulate the colours he paints his material with, mastering their tonalities, knowing where to place them and in what amounts, and how to mix them and arrange them, achieves what his fellow-painters fail to achieve, for his painting turns out more wonderful and more original.

The same difference exists between one poet and another 'as regards the meaning which both are aiming at'.[6]

Just as literary excellence is not to be found in the words of a text taken in isolation, nor in the meaning, neither is it to be found in the poet's knowledge of the language and its current usages. For if this were the case:

> then his innovative use of language in inventing metaphors and figures of speech would not constitute literary excellence. If merit is only judged to lie in the use of a metaphor already well known and used in the language of the Arabs, then ignorance has gone too far! Literary excellence lies in choosing well and knowing how to arrange the words . . . If discourse is like illumination and gold- and silver-work, and meaning is like the material which is being worked on — such as the silver and gold from which a ring or a bracelet is made — then it would be absurd for us, if we wanted to judge the way the ring was made and the excellence or otherwise of its craftsmanship, to consider the silver or gold in which it was worked. In the same way, it is absurd, if we want to know where excellence and superiority of poetical speech lie, to consider only its meaning.[7]

Two points emerge from the above: first, that poeticalness comes from the way that meaning is established, and second, that this poeticalness is not only discovered by listening — it is necessary to study the text 'with the heart . . . aided by the intellect', 'to reflect upon it, to consult reason and to have recourse to intelligence'.[8]

If we were to have asked al-Jurjānī, in this context, 'What about metre?' he would have answered, 'Metre is of no concern to us.' The claims he makes for poetry are not on account of its metre, but on account of the apt use of simile, metaphor, suggestion and allusion, and a particular and unique artistic skill.[9] Metre:

> has nothing to do with eloquence and rhetoric. Otherwise two poems with the same metre would be equal in their eloquence and the power of their rhetoric. For it is not metre that makes poetic discourse what it is, nor makes one poem better than another.[10]

If composition is the secret of poeticalness, what is the secret of composition? According to al-Jurjānī it is the figurative use of language (*majāz*): 'The beauties of discourse derive on the whole from the art of metaphor and the figures connected with it.'[11] Metaphorical language is 'magic', he says. Through it poetical speech is constantly renewed; 'It gives you an abundance of meanings in the simplest of words'; 'The inanimate comes to life and speaks, and mute bodies become eloquent.' It shows you 'subtle meanings — secrets of the mind — as if they had been made flesh', and refines 'physical characteristics until they become spiritual and can only be grasped by intuition'.[12]

Metaphor (*isti^cāra*) itself is the highest stage of this figurative language. An image has no power to agitate or provoke unless a similarity is established between two things which differ in kind. The more extreme the distance between the two things compared, the stranger the image appears and the more delight it arouses in the soul. An image is admired when through it a person can see two things as like and unlike, harmonious and divergent. Metaphor performs a magic operation, 'bringing a harmony to the unharmonious as if shortening the distance between East and West, making opposites agree, and uniting life and death, fire and water'.[13] In doing this it lets us enter a world of 'strangeness', as al-Jurjānī calls it, where poetic images cannot be grasped quickly by the mind and do not take shape in the imagination at a mere glance. They can only be grasped:

> after corroborating, remembering, searching with a fine

> toothcomb for familiar images, stimulating the imagination to visualize them and summon up those which are absent.[14] . . . All obvious similarity, related to external appearance or description, can be perceived at any time, and so a simile constructed from it will be trivial and banal. The opposite process, as different from the other as it can be, makes the simile strange, rare and new. Similes are rated according to where they stand in relation to these extremes: those closest to the first are the most banal, and those closest to the second the most sublime, and because of their strangeness, the most innovative.[15]

The principle behind all this is to create a synthesis of things which are different, or more precisely, 'extreme convergence in extreme divergence'.[16]

Al-Jurjānī explains why metaphorical language is admired, saying that 'Human nature is constructed in such a way that if a thing appears from an unexpected place, or emerges from an unfamiliar source, the soul admires it with a greater passion.'[17]

But how can we recognize excellence in poetry? How can we discover the finer points of poetic technique, 'the places where skill and mastery are located', as al-Jurjānī puts it? In answer to these questions, al-Jurjānī indicates that:

> there is no mystery or problem that is stranger, more oddly obscure or harder to grasp intellectually than the concept of excellence in poetry. The terms used to characterize it by rhetoricians and other scholars are symbols, incomprehensible to anyone who is not as subtle as them, and is less well prepared to understand what these signs mean . . . Meaning in poetry . . . is like the pearl in a shell; it does not emerge unless you crack open the shell and extract it . . . Not every thought will lead to the discovery of what it contains, nor every idea be permitted

to reach it: not everyone will succeed in splitting open the shell, thereby becoming one of the people of knowledge.[18]

The images invented by metaphorical language 'hint at things pictured by the imagination' and not understood except by 'instinctive reason and the vision of the heart'. They are subtle and delicate, obscure and unfamiliar, so that they can only be understood by a form of interpretation which relies on deep contemplation, reflection and subtlety of thought. Only those whose intellect and vision make them out of the ordinary can understand them properly; that is 'those with pure intellects, sharp minds, sound natures and souls ready to perceive wisdom'.[19]

It is essential to understand the details of poetic technique, because 'in understanding the details, preference is given to a certain way of looking, a certain way of listening; while for a general understanding the approach is undifferentiated'. When we perceive a particular detail we see it or hear it and derive pleasure from it, selecting it from the mass of others and distinguishing it from them. But when we take no interest in detail, it is as if we treat poetry as nonsense and thus debase it.[20]

Just as there are degrees of skill in the understanding of poetry, so there are degrees of technical ability in composing it. Poets are ranked in accordance with the subtlety of their manner of creating imagery. Some are then granted the status of 'the skilled craftsman, the inspired, the brilliant innovator who has been first to produce some type of creation, so that you know that creation by his name',[21] while others are called apprentices and imitators, who improve on their models, knowing that blind imitation is a defect.[22]

If in addition to this we remember that for al-Jurjānī general meanings and common matters have no poetic distinction, and that this is a quality that has to be discovered by thought, or is in what he calls 'the meaning of the meaning' — that is, that from the literal meaning of a word which we grasp at once, we are led to another meaning — we may deduce that he sees poetry and the understanding of poetry as specialist activities, restricted to people of sensitivity and knowledge.[23]

In conclusion, al-Jurjānī's criticism, to which I have referred briefly only in so far as it concerns the present discussion, refutes almost completely the poetic criteria of pre-Islamic orality and establishes other criteria for a poetics of writing, taking inspiration from the horizons opened up for the written word by the text of the Qur'ān.

It is clear from the above that modernity in Arabic poetry in particular, and in the written language in general, has its roots in the Qur'ān; the poetics of pre-Islamic orality represents the ancient in poetry, while Quranic studies laid the foundations of a new textual criticism, indeed invented a new science of aesthetics, thus paving the way for the growth of a new Arab poetics.

If, moreover, we take account of the Qur'ān's influence on the poetic quality of the writings of the mystics, we can see how the written language of the Qur'ān gave birth to a new appreciation of artistic language and to its practical application in a new kind of writing, and how the Qur'ān became 'the wellspring of literature', in the words of Ibn al-Athīr (1162–1239). In this way Quranic studies have provided the most important source for the study of the poetical qualities of the Arabic language.

Before indicating those aspects of modernity which first appeared in the Qur'ān and attempting to sum them up in a few general principles, I should like to refer to some of the poets who, from the middle of the ninth century onwards, began to apply in their poetry the theories formulated in textual studies of the Qur'ān. Muslim Ibn al-Walīd (d. 823) was the first to attempt to make the rhetoric of poetry similar to that of the Qur'ān — as al-Rummānī defines it, 'to communicate the meaning to the heart by way of the most vivid image'. According to Ibn Qutayba, Ibn al-Walīd was 'the first to make meanings subtle and speech delicate'. He was also, according to others, the first to rely on *badī*[c] (the art of using figures of speech: metaphor, antithesis, assonance), being inspired to do so by the Quranic text.

Bashshār Ibn Burd (714–84) was one of the first poets to attack the poetics of pre-Islamic orality and to invent a language of written poetics, or a language of the city instead of a language of the desert. With Abū Nuwās (757–814) this language reached an unprecedented peak of technical achievement, resulting in an almost complete transformation of the language of poetry. The beginning of the modern in written poetics is represented in Abū Nuwās's poetry in its richest and most complex and comprehensive forms, an epistemological approach to things and the world and humanity, with a new sensibility and a new aesthetics.

The poet Abū Tammām started out from a vision of poetry as a sort of creation of the world through language, comparing the relationship between the poet and the word to the relationship between two lovers, and the act of composing poetry to the sexual act. So in his poetry he constructs unfamiliar relationships between one word and another, between the word and the object, and between the human being and the world, thus upsetting the accustomed distinction between words and meaning, and the prevailing oral-based concept of poetry itself.

I shall now summarize the aesthetic and critical principles which were developed under the influence of Quranic studies and which formed the basis of the transition from the poetics of pre-Islamic orality to a written poetics.

Poetry should be written without reference to any previously existing model. This principle meant that the poet not only had to avoid imitating pre-Islamic poetry, but also had to break new ground in ways of expression, in exploring his own soul, and in his approach to inanimate things and to the world about him. This view of poetry as a beginning, not an imitation, ecouraged the formulation of critical terms and concepts all of which affirmed individuality and innovation. Bashshār Ibn Burd was called the 'master of the moderns' and was said to have 'travelled a road which no one else had travelled'. Abū Tammām was described as 'the head of the body of poesy', 'the leader of a school', an 'inventor' whose poetry was 'a miracle' — his disciple and friend, al-Buḥturī, called him 'the leader and master', and others described him as 'the imam who is followed'. Abū'l-ᶜAlā' al-Maᶜarrī (973–1057) named the poetry of al-Mutanabbī (915–65) 'Aḥmad's miracle'. (One of al-Mutanabbī's names was Aḥmad, and it is also an alternative name for the Prophet.)

This principle also involved an insistence on the continual violation of established practice in order that poetry should always be strange and new in its language, structures, images and meanings.

A vast cultural knowledge should be a prerequisite for every poet and critic. The reading and writing of poetry demand knowledge, expertise and intellectual discipline. Natural ability, skill in improvisation and mere linguistic knowledge are not enough. This principle led to the notion that poetry is not for everybody: its appreciation and practice are confined to a special group and it is difficult for those who are not of this group to understand it.

All texts, whether ancient or modern, should be examined without reference to the time of their composition and evaluated according to their intrinsic artistic value.

In this principle there is the beginning of a recognition that perfection is not the monopoly of the ancient and that the modern is not necessarily inferior to it. Indeed, it is possible for the modern to be more beautiful. The ancient is therefore no longer a critical standard or a model of poetic beauty.

This resulted in certain specific elements of poetry being emphasized while others diminished in importance. Al-Jurjānī, for example, as we have seen, attaches less importance to metre for its own sake, and al-Baqillānī stresses the unity of the poem and the unity of the Quranic sura in his analyses of these two forms. The texture of the work was also studied in much greater detail. Words and meaning were no longer thought of as distinct; the point was stressed that a word is not ugly or beautiful in itself: its ugliness or beauty depends upon its context and the way it is made to relate to the other words around it. Similarly, eloquence does not lie in the individual words which are used, but in the particular ways they are woven together and the artistic and semantic relationships constructed by this fabric of words.

A new conception of what constituted beauty in the poetic text was evolved.
The clarity of the pre-Islamic oral tradition was no longer a standard of beauty capable of arousing passion. On the contrary, al-Jurjānī and others came to see it as the antithesis of what was poetical. True poetic beauty was to be found in ambiguous, difficult texts which permitted a variety of interpretations and offered a multiplicity of meanings, texts which 'the spirit can approach in all manner of ways', as al-Rummānī expresses it.

The dynamic nature of creativity and experimentation was acknowledged and given precedence over the unchanging rules of the ancient texts.
Poetry appears as a continual transcending of what is ordinary, shared, handed down and 'is not afraid to violate the consensus', as al-Jurjānī puts it. Poetic writing is 'a kind of sedition', in his words again, or:

> an alchemy which gives a doubtful argument the authority of proof, and turns proof back into a doubtful argument; makes contemptible material into something original and of great value; inverts essences, transforms natures, so that the claims of alchemy are justified and the dreams of the elixir come true — except that this alchemy is spiritual, clothed in imagination and intellect, not body and matter.[24]

Perhaps the best way to end, and to express the range of the new poetics, is to quote these lines of Abū Nuwās, which are a poetic statement in themselves:

> But I say what comes to me
> From my inner thoughts
> Denying my eyes.
> I begin to compose something
> In a single phrase
> With many meanings,
> Standing in illusion,
> So that when I go towards it
> I go blindly,
> As if I am pursuing the beauty of something
> Before me but unclear.

3
Poetics and Thought

I should like to begin this lecture on Arab poetics and thought by noting three factors. The first relates to Arabic literary criticism, the second to the epistemological system based on the Arab-Islamic linguistic and religious sciences (grammar, rhetoric, jurisprudence, theology), and the third to the purely philosophical system.

1. As previously mentioned, literary criticism for the most part took pre-Islamic poetry as a model and an ideal and evaluated subsequent poetry according to how closely it adhered to its poetic method. This criticism was based on the assumption that pre-Islamic poetry was the depository not only of Arab songs and music but also of truths and knowledge, which implied that the pre-Islamic poets not only sang or recited, but 'thought' in their poetry as well, and that it was therefore a source of knowledge and not simply of musical pleasure. Put another way, pre-Islamic poetry was not uniform but plural. The problem arose when this plurality was compressed into a single model, viewed by the critics simply as 'song'. Thus the values peculiar to song and recitation became predominant in pre-Islamic poetry, and subsequently the criteria of poetic orality were the ones most often applied in appraising poetry. As a result, poetry and thought were definitively separated. When the purveyors of this critical

viewpoint considered that a certain poet inclined to 'thought' in some form or another, they judged his poetry to be a deviation from what they termed 'the Arab method' of composing poetry. This deviation was known variously as vagueness (*ghumūḍ*), complexity (*taᶜqīd*), exaggerated strangeness (*ighrāb*) or that which is absurd (*muḥāl*), that is, that which deviates from the 'truth'. All these descriptions were applied regardless of the poetical value of the work in question, and there were those critics who did not even define Abū'l-ᶜAlā' al-Maᶜarrī as a poet, preferring to call him 'the sage'. Al-Mutanabbī before him had been assigned a similar status, and earlier still Abū Tammām was described as a 'corrupter' of Arabic poetry and of 'the method of the Arabs'.

Such criticism failed to acknowledge that the work of these later poets, by virtue of the fact that thought plays a part in it, constitutes a continuation in one form or another of pre-Islamic poetry itself, and one which is naturally richer and more varied than the earlier tradition.[1] The critics also seemed to forget that it was they themselves who had repeated many times over that poetry for the Arabs was not only 'an anthology of songs', but 'a collection of their knowledge', 'a witness to their right behaviour and their wrongdoing', 'a source which they return to' (Ibn Khaldūn); that in it lay 'truth and wisdom', that it was 'a harvest of the fruits of the intellect', 'a leader and a guide', 'a cultured preacher' and a force for 'immortalizing the legacy of the past' (al-Jurjānī). In short, they forgot that pre-Islamic poetry, in addition to being song, is a particular way of approaching the world and things through thought, based on an intellectual experience as well as an emotional one.

2. The epistemological system which was built upon religion (jurisprudence and theology) on the one hand, and language (grammar and rhetoric) on the other, also made an unequivocal division between poetry and thought. The paradox here is that

what religion had considered to be error and temptation was turned by the partisans of this system into a source of aesthetic enjoyment and spiritual pleasure. This system, derived from a written text with all the characteristics peculiar to writing — the Qur'ān — itself gave support to the theorizing of sung orality and reinforced its artistic criteria, thus helping to proclaim them as fixed, almost absolute, standards.

3. The epistemological system based on philosophical argumentation represents in one sense a complete break with the two above, in terms of its methodology and its approach to knowledge. In its conception of poetry, however, it is paradoxically a continuation or even a completion of these two systems, adding to their arguments its own particular arguments, drawn from Greek thought.

Thus we see that poetry in the eyes of most Arab theoreticians was either an object of 'pleasure and musical delight', or something to be 'banished and rejected': it operated either in the sphere of the untrue and the absurd, or in that of sensuous enjoyment. In other words, the poetical was a defective or negative way of approaching the world and its mysteries; at best, poetry could be described as a game, as mimesis or representation, but it had nothing to do with the search for knowledge.

From a religious point of view, it is possible to find a justification for what the religious-linguistic system affirms. If we go back to the root of the Arabic word for poetry (*shiᶜr*), that is to the verb *shaᶜara*, we see that it means 'to know', 'to understand' and 'to perceive'. On this basis, all knowledge is poetry. We call the poet *shāᶜir* (literally, 'one who knows, understands, perceives') in Arabic because he perceives and understands (*yashᶜuru*) that which others do not perceive and understand, that is he knows (*yaᶜlamu*) what others do not know.[2] But in general the term 'poetry' (*shi^{c}r*) is used for a type of speech regulated by metre and rhyme, speech 'defined by markings which are not to be violated', and the verb *sha^{c}ara* has come most often to have another meaning: 'to feel'. Thus poetry has become feeling, and that 'with which we express the beginning of knowledge of perceived things'. This is why people say, 'I feel feverish,' but not 'I feel that God is one,' for God is not 'felt' but 'realized' or 'grasped'. Perhaps this offers an explanation in religious terms as to why poetry is confined to sensation, and why the separation is made between poetry and thought. Poetry is not to go beyond the first stages of knowledge: such is the function accorded to sensation. What does go beyond sensation is religion, and it was on the basis of this idea that poetry came to be widely seen as by definition incapable of presenting knowledge or revealing truth. It is, like its starting-point sensation, treacherous and worthless. Only through religion, not poetry, can we perceive the truth. The role of poetry is therefore limited to providing aesthetic pleasure, within the bounds set and deemed permissible by religion.

This goes against the original meaning of the word which allows us to call into question the accepted usage of the term 'poetry' and to unite poetry and thought, for poetry is not content with feeling things, but thinks about them also.

Even if we can find a justification for the attitude adopted by the linguistic-religious system towards poetry, what justification is there for the attitude of literary criticism itself? The truth is that this criticism perverted the research into poetics at a fundamental level: it was not criticism of the poetry for its own sake, but of its functional and socio-ethical connections. The critical awareness was, strictly speaking, functional rather than poetical. In particular it was on the question 'What is poetry?' and the precisely defined answer to this question that the critic based his appreciation and judgement of poetry.

The questions raised by these three factors require a special study in themselves. At the very least we need to reread our critical-intellectual heritage, and in the light of this rewrite the history of Arabic poetry and its aesthetics.

What is missing from the theory can be found in the creative text. Such a text, examples of which are found in the work of some poets and mystics, transcends these epistemological systems and their theories. It achieves in its structure and its vision an organic relationship between poetry and thought, and by its insights and moments of illumination it opens up before us a new aesthetic horizon, and also a new horizon of thought.

This text arises basically from a vision which does not divide a human being into two distinct parts — thought and feeling, or emotion and intellect — but considers him as an indivisible whole, a force of unified consciousness. Because of its distinguishing features, this written text stands at the opposite extreme from the oral text. The mystical text, in particular, was responsible for creating a new poetical language and form which exists alongside metric poetry and is independent of it.

I shall give three examples to illustrate the unity of poetry and thought in Arab creative writing, examples which are varied enough to offer a more or less faithful picture; they are the texts of Abū Nuwās, al-Niffarī (d. 965) and Abū'l-ᶜAlā' al-Maᶜarrī.

Abū Nuwās

The writing of Abū Nuwās may be considered a debut, but an almost perfect debut, based on this unity of poetry and thought. Its underlying motif is the dialectic between what the poet rejects and what he accepts and commends. He rejects the values of bedouin life, and he rejects religious dogmatism, especially its moral aspect. He advocates urban life and values, and calls for the dogma to be transcended and taboos disregarded. There is scarcely a poem of his where this dialectic is absent; it is always directed towards a synthesis depicting some aspect of human life or intellectual activity which the poet wants to open up. Thus we perceive a method constantly at work behind the text, directed towards a particular kind of knowledge and a particular moral order. The poetical element is to be found in the exploration of human potential and frustrated human desires, and in the unleashing of these desires in such a way that the gap separating emotion and action, desire and ability, is eliminated. It is also present in what is implied by this unleashing: the destruction of the walls barring the way to the wide open spaces of freedom. In Abū Nuwās's poetry there is a flame which devours every obstacle, be it social or religious. For him, joy does not come from the practice of the permissible but, on the contrary, from the pursuit of the forbidden and the illicit. He considers that the violation of taboos gives rise to a disordered state of bliss which is the equivalent of destroying the existing cultural and ethical systems, and which holds in it a firm promise of the advent of a culture in which there will be no repression and no restrictions. This new culture will take a stand against the old values of 'Thou shalt' and 'Thou shalt not', and allow life to be lived in such a way that a harmony is created between the rhythms of the body and the rhythms of reality in a music of freedom.

Abū Nuwās adopts the mask of a clown and turns drunkenness, which frees bodies from the control of logic and traditions, into a symbol of total liberation. This symbol is a vast crucible of metamorphoses. Wine is not wine: it is a symbol and an indicator, a force which transforms, annihilates, constructs, rejects and affirms. It is the ancient creator, to which everything is related, but which itself is related to nothing. It is the beginning of life and the eternal return, and between the two it is life in one of its most splendid meanings: love. It is a life-changing power, which reconciles opposites and makes the ordinary logic of time meaningless. It is the intoxication of the encounter with the self, and of the joining of the self with the world. As the Creator is the essence of the universe, and the world is a forest of signs representing His names, characteristics and deeds, so wine is also an essence, and the things of the world a tissue of correspondences between it and the universe. Wine is fire, a living being which speaks and sees; the glasses which hold it are lamps and stars; the gathering where it is consumed is a celestial sphere where people die and are born again. The descent into the depths of the soul is at the same time a descent into the depths of nature.

If this symbol represents the violation of the taboo in such a way that everything becomes permissible on the level of values, then in the sphere of knowledge it represents the exploration of the unknown, both in the self and in the natural world. It is an indication that the visible is the face of the invisible, and the tangible the threshold of the intangible, the point at which the divisions disappear and the surface meaning and the inner sense become one. Just as it takes a person out of the place where he is and transports him to another, secret place, so also it lifts him from the present moment into a beyond where life is transformed into an eternity of elation.

Thus the insolence of the clown purifies and liberates. It is a celebration which holds in it the promise of something capable of going beyond this culture of orders and prohibitions to a culture of freedom, in which human beings will be masters and mistresses of their thoughts, actions and conduct. Values are transformed through this symbol and sin becomes the only virtue. We hear the voice of Abū Nuwās telling us that he has no desire to commit the sins of ordinary people, but aspires to sins equal in stature to the liberation which he is striving for, grand sins 'which will eclipse all others', as he puts it. He preaches rebellion against 'the tyrant of the skies' and proclaims that 'pleasure is in the forbidden things', that 'the pilgrimage (*ḥajj*) is a visit to the publican' and that 'his proud spirit scorns to be satisfied with anything but prohibited joys'. 'My religion is for myself! Other people's religion is for other people!' he cries. Through sin itself he will acquire innocence.

Al-Niffarī

The transcendental or the invisible — the area of revelation — is al-Niffarī's subject, and one which he attempts to explore in detail. But however much progress he makes, his efforts only convince him of the need to go still further. What he succeeds in finding out is only at the threshold of all that remains unknown and calls to him to discover it; it is as if, as he comes to know more, he says to himself, 'I know that I do not know.' To find expression, this experience requires discourse which frees itself from everyday usage, and from reason and logic at the same time. It belongs in the realm of things which are not said. Language in this context is a daring attempt to say what is not said.

All this drives him to progress beyond the known. As he progresses he renews himself constantly so that he is always present and ready to keep going along the way of discovery.

Between speech and silence where there is the gulf which contains 'the tomb of reason and the cemetery of things', as al-Niffarī expresses it, moves his text, silent in its speech, articulate in its silence. He employs language not to express himself in words — for they are powerless — but to express himself in the relationships that he can weave from them in the form of symbols and signs. His language is essentially metaphorical. It extracts the significance of a word from its rational context and places it in a context accessible only through interpretation. That is why the words seem submerged by the indefinable. What they transmit is not in them but in what they hide. It is as if, paradoxically, they express what cannot be expressed.

Al-Niffarī gives a subjective dimension to religion, thereby laying the foundations of another epistemological outlook, different from the traditional religious one. By his hermeneutic approach to the text of the Qur'ān he caused an upheaval in the way it was regarded. In both cases he transports us from the surface to the inner meaning, and from rational knowledge to sensuous and intuitive knowledge. By affirming subjective experience he eliminates the normative. There are no models in al-Niffarī's text: it is a text-source. As it depicts an experience which is not repeated, it remains in a state of perpetual renewal, and this is what makes it a text bound to infinity. In this affirmation of the subjective the problem changes. According to the literalist view, it was, 'How shall I act so that my conduct and my thinking comply with the law?' but it becomes, 'Who am I? How shall I know myself and know the truth?'

In this way al-Niffarī's text appears to be a complete break with tradition in its various forms and manifestations; with it he renews Arab creative energy and the language of poetry simultaneously. He writes history following the vision of his heart and intoxicated by language, and raises poetic writing to a level unknown before, in the most sublime and original ways allowed by the language. In his writing, for the first time in Arabic literature, we see human anguish and thirst and questioning expressed, like the crashing of waves as the tide ebbs and flows, an interchange of absence and presence in an eternity of light.

Perhaps the most profound characteristic of the poetical nature of this text is that the explosion of thought in it is nothing short of an explosion of language itself. In delivering thought from its blind alley, al-Niffarī delivers language too. He liberates both of them from functionalism and rationalism and restores to both their essential mission: to go deep into the self and human existence and explore them in all their dimensions. This outburst of thought and language is full of sudden illuminations and tensions conflicting and merging, in such a way that the text seems to flood out on to the stage of the self in images which engage and disengage, and move together and apart, outside all causality, as if they were dreams. The words of the text appear to say themselves, whispering together, debating, clashing and harmonizing in a beautiful, captivating frenzy, as if the text is playing a game with itself and with existence, a game whose splendour and nobility are without precedent, as if language is itself the motion of being, fused into vowels and consonants, or is inextricable from the movement of experience. Thought is pure poetry, and poetry pure thought.

Al-Niffarī's text places us in a unique world of incandescent bliss. It is the text as bliss. When reading it we feel that we emerge from the oppressive conditions of our lives and embrace salvation. It eliminates the gap between the human and the sacred, humanizing the sacred and sanctifying this thinking, poeticizing reed: the human being.

He tells us, however, that the transcendental cannot be known; it remains essentially a longing for the transcendental. Just as longing provokes speech, so speech arouses longing and transforms it into a longing for its source: the transcendental, which from time to time emits a gleam of light, but remains hidden, remote and incomprehensible. In this permanent state of unfulfilment we discover a paradox through al-Niffarī's text: the truth only exists in all its clarity, that is in all its obscurity, in an experience such as this existential union where thought is poetry and poetry thought.

Al-Ma^{c}arrī

Al-Ma^{c}arrī subjects the beliefs and ideas of his age to a process of questioning in which thought wears the guise of poetry and poetry has the power of thought. In other words, he puts them in an intellectual framework which is charged with poetic sensibility and influenced by numerous different psychological factors. When we read al-Ma^{c}arrī, we enter a field of contemplation where the poet shows us that he has many voices, although this pluralism is not enough to explain his text. The knowledge with which it overflows is in direct contrast to the kind of knowledge based on eternal verities, religious knowledge in particular. Thus he exposes those things which were suppressed at the time in which he lived, and urges thought on matters which do not yield themselves up easily to thought. He is a symbol of the departure from all kinds of sectarianism and established truths of whatever persuasion. His poetry gives the impression of casting the reader into a climate of loss, or even nihilism, as the essential nature of the world.

If poetry was, according to the 'method of the Arabs', 'the art of words', al-Ma^{c}arrī makes it into the art of meaning. To be more precise, we could say that al-Ma^{c}arrī's text is an encounter between words we possess and meanings we are searching for. However this is a search which always leads to doubt and confusion. Al-Ma^{c}arrī establishes nothing, at the level of either language or meaning. On the contrary, all that he proposes only casts doubt on both of these: for him they are simply two ways of expressing futility and nothingness. He creates his world — if create is the right word — with death as his starting-point. Death is the one elixir, the redeemer. Life itself is only a death running its course. A person's clothes are his shroud; his house is his grave, his life his death, and his death his true life. In a variation on the theme, the poet says that a man's native land is a prison, death is his release from it, and the grave alone is secure. Therefore the best thing for him is to die like a tree which is pulled up by the roots and leaves neither roots nor branches behind it. Humanity is unadulterated filth and the earth cannot be purified unless mankind ceases to exist. The truth is that the most evil of trees is the one which has borne human beings. Life is a sickness whose cure is death. Death is a celebration of life. Man smells sweeter when he is dead, as musk when it is crushed releases all of its aroma. Moreover, the soul has an instinct for death, a perpetual desire to become wedded to it.

Al-Ma^{c}arrī's text reveals the original absence in life. To put it another way, life is by its nature absent. Time, in all its rotten presence, is no more than a joke. Man's birth is an original sin, for life is originally corrupt.

So why poetry? It is there to remind us of all this, and so that each of us will be able to say with al-Ma^{c}arrī:

> My body is a rag to be sewn to the earth.
> O you who sews worlds, sew me!

The poetry of Abū Nuwās, al-Niffarī and al-Ma^{c}arrī can be characterized as a product of thought and imagination combined. The element of thought is there in so far as the texts go beyond the areas of knowledge of the time and generate a feeling of epistemological anguish *vis-à-vis* religion, established values and morals, God and the supernatural, life and death, and all the other problems which humanity confronts. It is poetry which proceeds from an obsessive desire to discover the truth and to know the self and the world.

It is not a product of the imagination, as a purely psychological or sensory faculty, but in the mystical sense, especially as it is manifested in al-Niffarī's poetry. In this sense, the imagination is an intermediary between the spirit which belongs to the transcendental world and the senses which belong to the world of tangible evidence. It is also a depository from which the spirit draws its primary material. It is creative energy, free and unlimited, and a light which allows transfigurations to be glimpsed by piercing the veil of darkness that hides things. Because it is light, it does not err. Error is begotten by judgement and the imagination does not pass judgement. Error occurs in reason, the faculty which produces judgements, and which can err in its understanding of those things revealed by the imagination. That is why it is impossible to evaluate the mystical text rationally: it is the product of an experience in which reason and its judgements have no place.

It is in the eye of the imagination that the symbolic images are formed, which should lead us to a perception of the truths symbolized by them. The imagination resembles a womb: as the foetus is formed in the womb, meanings are formed in the imagination and materialize in various images. In this way the imagination conveys us from the known to the unknown.

While there is no appreciable gap between the poetics and the thought in the texts of Abū Nuwās and al-Niffarī, the poetry of al-Ma^{c}arrī is often weighed down by a sort of cold intellectualism, overlaid by its nightmarish qualities. T.S. Eliot's observation that 'Blake's poetry has the unpleasantness of great poetry' applies also to al-Ma^{c}arrī's writing. To call it unpleasant does not mean that it is sick, or complex and without passion, but rather that it holds its reader constantly over a chasm of absurdity and nothingness.

On another level, we could describe these three examples of the creative text as representing an approach to things and mankind where psychological influences are much involved and reason and logic are kept at a distance. In them meaning is expressed in a symbolic structure. There is no separation between what we call feeling and what we call contemplation and awareness. Poetry here is an existential vision and a spiritual, meditative experience. It is an act of reflection and illumination whose instruments are neither tradition nor reason, neither argumentation nor logic; they are intuition, insight, the eye of the heart.

If we now go back to the root of the word *fikr* (thought), we will see that it originally concerned the soul and the heart, and not reason. It was connected with the actions of the heart or mind (*khāṭir*) in its approach to the object. *Khāṭir* also signifies a feeling or an idea or a notion that passes through the heart. Therefore to think (*fakara*) is to contemplate with the heart.

The word *ᶜaql* (reason) was originally connected with morals, for it was reason which prevented the reasonable being from abandoning himself to his passions. It restrained him (one of the basic meanings of the root *ᶜaqala*), protecting him from moral peril. Accordingly, thought is a blend of intuition and reflection.

If we consider poetry as intuition of the mind and spirit combined, it will be clear that the separation between poetry and thought goes back, on another level, to the view that poetry is misleading, not only because it relies on unreliable senses, but because it thinks in a manner which is not governed by any particular system. It thinks in symbols and images, which systems of knowledge cannot encompass and are incapable of explaining completely, despite their claims to be comprehensive.

Hence we can understand how disturbing the 'creative text' was for those who adhered to the religious and rational systems of knowledge. On the one hand it offers a kind of knowledge not incorporated into their systems, and impossible to acquire by the means which they use; and on the other, it proves the absurdity of the notion of a complete vision or total knowledge, on which these systems claim to be founded. Moreover the knowledge in this text is dynamic, explosive and unfettered. It is a dislocation, an experimentation. It is not based on analysis or logic or a preordained method, but on the person, his experience, his vitality and his capability. The world appears in the text as an infinity of empty spaces and focuses of action, of disorder and diversity. There is no stability, and nothing in thought is pre-established.

The creative text does in fact deal with religious and philosophical questions, but in its own specific way and with its own manner of expression. It reveals points of view and opinions which upset the systems of both the religious and the philosophical approach. Unlike the philosophical and religious texts, it has nothing to do with what has already been thought, either in terms of the experiences it portrays or the discoveries it makes. On the contrary, it enters areas of thought which have not been entered before, which are suppressed or remain hidden and remote. It reveals truths by a method which employs neither belief nor rational argumentation, a method which offers a knowledge of the thing itself, and which is far removed from the sort of knowledge offered by either the religious or the philosophical method.

We would add that the knowledge in this text is not about certainties, nor is it an answer, as is the case with the knowledge offered by religion or philosophy. On the contrary, it is a questioning. In the Arab-Islamic epistemological tradition, thought is an answer, and as poetry offers no answers it is therefore defined as being entirely separate from thought. But while the poet does not provide an answer, this is not to say that he does not think: as poetry is a questioning, it leaves the horizon open to inquiry and further knowledge; it offers no certainties. Questioning is thought, giving rise to anguish and doubt, while answering is a sort of cessation from thought, bringing confidence and certainty. Questioning, in other words, is thought which provokes more thought.

Finally, this text allows us to define the element of thought in poetry on four levels:

1. The poetic image in the creative text reveals the ambiguous and the obscure in a human being. It exposes what the reader feels or thinks, but has not made any previous attempt to know, thereby presenting him with the means to perceive his internal world more clearly and understand it better.

2. This poetic image reveals the basic contours of the external world, thus conveying what is suppressed, unknown or ignored.

By its manner of demonstrating these existing realities, the text begets questions which point to other realities, and thus broadens the range of knowledge and experience.

3. These revelations and questionings shift, as they are read, out of the framework of personal emotions to become more comprehensive; features of the poetry with purely aesthetic justifications are transformed and incorporated into the wider context of life and thought. What was personal and particular becomes general and universal.

4. Among these revelations are some which are so sublime that they become a key to the unknown, or a foundation for new, unforeseen visions. They are not only a help in understanding existing realities, but also allow us to construct a point of departure for perceiving the future. As they illuminate existence and the human soul, they also offer possibilities for thought and action.

It remains for me to discuss the essential characteristic of the creative text, which is the language. In the language, poetry and thought are fused into a unity of consciousness, in such a way that thought seems to emanate from the poetry like perfume from a rose. This characteristic is embodied in the metaphorical structure of the expression.

'Most of language', writes the linguistician Ibn Jinnī, 'is metaphorical, not literal. Metaphor is a deviation from the use of language in its true sense, that is according to its original designation.'[3]

The switch from literal to figurative language takes place for the following reasons: extension of meaning, emphasis and comparison. Metaphor in Arabic is more than an expressional device; it is in the structure of the language itself, an indication of a spiritual need to transcend reality, that is the immediate and the given, and the product of a sensibility which is bored by the concrete and looks beyond it — a metaphysical sensibility. Metaphor transcends: just as the language of metaphor goes beyond itself to something less accessible, so it goes beyond the reality which it is talking about and enters less accessible areas. It is as if in its very nature metaphor is an act of rejection of existing reality and a search for an alternative.

Thus metaphor releases reality from its familiar context, while releasing the words used to discuss it from theirs, changing the meaning of both words and subject matter, and in the process constructing new relationships between one word and another, and between the word and reality.

Since metaphor frees words from their normal limits, the relationships which it establishes between words and reality are potential relationships; many meanings are possible within them, and this produces divergences in understanding, leading to divergences of opinion and evaluation. Metaphor does not allow a final and definitive answer, because it is in itself a battleground of semantic contradictions. It remains a begetter of questions, an agent of disruption, in contrast to the type of knowledge which aspires to certainty.

All this indicates that metaphor is linked to a vision of the truth. It is not only an attitude to the truth, but also a way of thinking about it, exploring it and expressing it.

If we add to this al-Jurjānī's opinion that 'Metaphor is always more eloquent than literalness,' then what is the status of religion and philosophy in a history of thought, that is in a history of truth written down in metaphorical language? From this question there emerges another aspect of the division between poetry and thought in Arab philosophy and religion. Both of these systems, each according to its particular approach, attach importance to what they call the truth, and to whatever has an obvious and definite meaning. In metaphor there is only probability, and so the religious system of knowledge characterizes it as a transferring of words away from their accepted meanings, and therefore a corruption of the words. This corruption harms the language because it gives rise to error and falsehood, the more so as God created each word to express its own particular meaning, and transferring the words means invalidating the truths which God has wanted us to perceive. The right way is to give each word the meaning originally laid down for it; the wrong way is to use it for a meaning other than that assigned to it. It is obvious that this dictum invalidates not only metaphor, but poetry as a whole.

It is clear, then, that there is a vast distance between the horizons of poetic knowledge and those of religious and philosophical knowledge. For these last two the meaning has to be expressed by the right word in order to be perfectly understood. But the former sees that if the spirit does not understand exactly what is meant by the words it will continue to long for complete understanding, whereas if the sense is immediately obvious, the yearning for perfection ceases to exist. The aim of what we know is to arouse a desire in us for what we do not know, a desire to increase our knowledge until it is perfect. Thus the world existing within the boundaries of religious and philosophical knowledge is closed and finite because it is certain; it becomes a system of beliefs and an ideology. But from the perspective of poetic, that is metaphoric, knowledge, the world is by contrast open and infinite, because it is possibility, a continuing process of search and discovery.

We can see at this point how Arabic, in its metaphoric or poetic structure, is a language which arouses a desire to search, to know the unknown and to attain perfection. It is too vast to be confined within the limits of the given and the actual: there is a dimension of infinity to its powers of expression, which corresponds to the non-finite aspects of knowledge.

This takes us on to the final point in this lecture which concerns the metaphoric element in the language of mysticism. Metaphor in relation to the experience of mysticism has no past. By this I mean that it is a perpetual beginning, a bridge connecting the seen and the unseen. As its aim is to reveal the unknown, the poetic image here does not take the form of a simile based on comparison and analogy, but is an invention created by the joining of two separate worlds into one. It is not merely a rhetorical or descriptive technique, but an original impulse, bursting into life in the same movement as poetic intuition. It refuses to be understood in rationalist or realist terms, because it has escaped from the limitations imposed by these two categories and refers to something beyond them. It is a penetrating, revealing light directed at the unknown. The image is a becoming, a change of state.

Mystical poetic writing is not therefore literature in the normal sense of the word, but another genre, difficult to define and codify. It is a perpetual act of discovery of the infinite, involving a constant destruction of forms. It does not remain settled in one form, because the form in this case, like the image, is an invention, which does not recur and cannot be constructed, adapted or copied. It is not a garment, an envelope or a vessel, but undulating space, the movement of feeling and thought, the rhythm of the heart. There is no form in the abstract for this kind of writing. Each poem has its own particular form.

We can see from the above that the writing of poetry is a reading of the world and the things in it, a reading of things charged with words, and of words tied to things. The mystery of poetry is that it remains a form of speech which goes against normal speech, so that it can give new names to things, seeing them in a new light. Language here does not only create the object; it creates itself in creating the object. Poetry is where the word transcends itself, escaping from the boundaries of its letters, and where the object takes on a new image and a different meaning. This is what is achieved in the kind of writing discussed above, although the works of Abū Nuwās, al-Niffarī and al-Ma^{c}arrī constitute a miniscule part of a huge body of writing, the significance of which we have only recently begun to understand, and which we are attempting to place in its proper aesthetic and epistemological framework.

4
Poetics and Modernity

We will only be able to reach a proper understanding of the poetics of Arab modernity by viewing it in its social, cultural and political context. Its development in the eighth century was bound up with the revolutionary movements demanding equality, justice and an end to discrimination between Muslims on grounds of race or colour. It was also closely connected with the intellectual movements engaged in a re-evaluation of traditional ideas and beliefs, especially in the area of religion.

The dominant view held that the state was founded on a vision or message which was Islam. On the one hand, this state was constituted as a caliphate, in which the designated successor not only followed on from his predecessor but preserved the heritage and conformed to it in both theory and practice; on the other hand, it was a state formed of a single community, meaning that unanimity of opinion was an essential requirement. Politics and thought were religious; religion was one and permitted no divergence.

This explains why for the most part those in power fought against these revolutionary and intellectual movements. Politically, they were considered as a rebellion against religion because they attacked the caliphate, which represented religious authority. From an intellectual and philosophical point of view, their adherents were seen as heretics and apostates, either for restricting the role of religion in the teaching of virtue, or for denying the role of revelation in knowledge and saying that knowledge and truth were the business of reason. The authorities viewed the mystical elements in these movements as constituting an attack on the law and practice of Islam; this was because they made a distinction between 'the evident' (*al-ẓāhir*) and 'the hidden' (*al-bāṭin*), or between 'the law' and 'the truth', asserting that knowledge and truth come from 'the hidden', hence the possibility of achieving a kind of unity or union between God and existence and between God and man.

To put it another way, those in power designated everyone who did not think according to the culture of the caliphate as 'the people of innovation' (*ahl al-iḥdāth*), excluding them with this indictment of heresy from their Islamic affiliation. This explains how the terms *iḥdāth* (innovation) and *muḥdath* (modern, new), used to characterize the poetry which violated the ancient poetic principles, came originally from the religious lexicon. Consequently we can see that the modern in poetry appeared to the ruling establishment as a political or intellectual attack on the culture of the regime and a rejection of the idealized standards of the ancient, and how, therefore, in Arab life the poetic has always been mixed up with the political and the religious, and indeed continues to be so.

The problematic of poetic modernity (*ḥadātha*) in Arab society goes beyond poetry in the narrow sense and is indicative of a general cultural crisis, which is in some sense a crisis of identity. This is linked both to an internal power struggle which has many different aspects and operates on various levels, and to an external conflict against foreign powers. It would appear that the return to the ancient has been more eagerly pursued whenever the internal conflict has intensified or the danger from outside has grown more acute. In Arab society today we find a powerful extension of this historical phenomenon which confirms our observation.

Perhaps this helps to explain why the current of modernity in Arab society sometimes flows strongly (as was the case in the eighth, ninth and tenth centuries) and at other times abates and recedes (as it did in the following centuries), according to whether the double-sided conflict, internal and external, is at a high or low point. It may also explain why modernity has tended to be a force which rejects, questions and provokes without entering in any conscious, radical way into the structure of the Arab mind or into Arab life as a whole. Perhaps, finally, it may go some way to explaining the dominance of the traditionalist mentality in Arab life and in Arabic poetry and thought.

The retreat of Arab society from the ways opened up by modernity began with the fall of Baghdad in 1258. With the Crusades came a complete halt, prolonged by the period of Ottoman domination.

From the beginning of the nineteenth century to the middle of the twentieth — the time of Western colonialism and of contact with its culture and its modernity, the period known as the *nahḍa* (renaissance, a name which merits a detailed study in itself) — the question of modernity was revived and the debate resumed over the issues which it provoked. Opinions were divided into two general tendencies: the traditionalist/conformist (*uṣūlī*) tendency, which considered religion and the Arab linguistic sciences as its main base; and the transgressing/non-conformist (*tajāwuzī*) tendency, which saw its base, by contrast, as lying in European secularism.

It is the first philosophy that has prevailed, especially at the level of the establishment, encouraged by economic, social and political conditions, both internal and external. According to this interpretation, the ancient — be it in religion, poetry or language — is the ideal of true and definitive knowledge. This implies that the future is contained within it: nobody who is a product of this culture is permitted to imagine the possibility of truths or knowledge being developed which would transcend this ancient ideal. According to this theory, modernity — as established in poetry by Abū Nuwās and Abū Tammām, in thought by Ibn al-Rāwandī (d. 910), al-Rāzī (d. 1210) and Jābir Ibn Hayyān (d. 815), and in the nature of visionary experience by the mystics, and which assumes the emergence of new truths about man and the world — is not only a criticism of the ancient but a refutation of it.

In other words, to believe in the pronouncements of modernity is to believe in things that have not been known before. Seen in this light, the new reveals a certain failing or lack in the old. Modernity therefore constitutes an attack on the fundamentals. On this basis we can understand the connection made between innovation in poetry, which violates the ancient, and heresy, and also why words like *ḥadīth* (modern) and *iḥdāth* (innovation), originally religious terms, could be carried over into the domain of poetry.

This traditionalist culture is embodied in the uninterrupted practice of an epistemological method which sees truth as existing in the text, not in experience or reality; this truth is given definitively and finally and there is no other. The role of thought is to explain and teach, proceeding from a belief in this truth, and not to search and question in order to arrive at new, conflicting truths.

It was therefore natural that this culture should reject a theory that was fundamentally opposed to it, especially those aspects of it which might have led people to doubt its religious vision and its cultural and intellectual apparatus.

Because of the dominance of this 'fundamentalist' knowledge at the level of the establishment and those in power, the Arabs find themselves — in spite of all the changes of the past fourteen centuries — moving on a stage where history is repeating itself with just one objective: the continual actualization of the past.

The reason this approach has gained in ascendancy is because 'modern' Arab thought has not confronted it in an analytical and critical manner and dismantled it completely. Perhaps it has not dared to, or perhaps it has preferred to work some kind of magic to make it vanish into thin air, which has quickly had the opposite effect. This may go some way towards explaining why 'modern' Arab thinkers have adapted to the shock of modernization from the West by treating modernity primarily as a technological achievement. For this reason modernity in Arab society has continued to be something imported from abroad, a modernity which adopts the new things but not the intellectual attitude and method which produced them, whereas true modernity is a way of seeing before it is production.

From an artistic and poetical point of view the dominance of traditionalist or fundamentalist culture led to a return to the values of pre-Islamic orality. Most of the poetry written after the so-called Arab renaissance (*nahḍa*), by such poets as al-Bārūdī (1838–1904), Shawqī (1882–1932) and their contemporaries, was no more than a ritual consolidation of this return. The poets who opposed the ancient, claiming to be modernizers, did not turn to Arab modernity as manifested in the poetry of Abū Nuwās and Abū Tammām or the mystic writings, nor did they refer to the theorization of the new poetic language carried out by al-Jurjānī. Instead, they began to imitate modern Western poetry.

Thus the crisis of modernity appeared at its most complex during the *nahḍa*, a period which created a split in Arab life, both theoretically and practically. On the one hand, it was a revival of forms of expression developed in past ages to respond to present problems and experiences, which was also a resuscitation of old ways of feeling and thinking and methods of approach. It therefore helped to establish these forms as absolute inviolable principles, to be eternally perpetuated as the single true poetry. The result was that the Arab personality, as expressed through this poetry, appeared to be a bundle of self-delusions, and Arab time to stand outside time. On the other hand, at the level of practical politics and daily life, the age of the *nahḍa* was set in motion in a state of almost complete dependency on the West.

In this way the period laid the foundations of a double dependency: a dependency on the past, to compensate for the lack of creative activity by remembering and reviving; and a dependency on the European-American West, to compensate for the failure to invent and innovate by intellectual and technical adaptation and borrowing. The present reality is that the prevailing Arab culture derives from the past in most of its theoretical aspects, the religious in particular, while its technique comes mainly from the West.

In both cases there is an obliteration of personality; in both cases, a borrowed mind, a borrowed life. This culture teaches not only the consumption of things but also the consumption of human beings.

Since the 1950s the cultural background of Arab poets and critics has derived from two divergent traditions: that of the self (ancient, traditionalist) and that of the other (modern, European-American). These two traditions blur or blot out the values of modernity and creativity in the Arab literary heritage. The first does so on the pretext of a return to original sources; the second does so perhaps out of ignorance, or is so dazzled by the other that it cannot perceive its own particular nature, and what distinguishes it from the other.

I should acknowledge here that I was one of those who were captivated by Western culture. Some of us, however, went beyond that stage, armed with a changed awareness and new concepts which enabled us to reread our heritage with new eyes and to realize our own cultural independence. I must also admit that I did not discover this modernity in Arabic poetry from within the prevailing Arab cultural order and its systems of knowledge. It was reading Baudelaire which changed my understanding of Abū Nuwās and revealed his particular poetical quality and modernity, and Mallarmé's work which explained to me the mysteries of Abū Tammām's poetic language and the modern dimension in it. My reading of Rimbaud, Nerval and Breton led me to discover the poetry of the mystic writers in all its uniqueness and splendour, and the new French criticism gave me an indication of the newness of al-Jurjānī's critical vision.

I find no paradox in declaring that it was recent Western modernity which led me to discover our own, older, modernity outside our 'modern' politico-cultural system established on a Western model.

The problem here is that the modern Arab poet sees himself in fundamental conflict both with the culture of the dominant political system, which reclaims the roots in a traditionalist manner, and with the images of Western culture as adapted and popularized by this system. The system separates us from our Arab modernity, from what is richest and most profound in our heritage. It is in collusion with the prevailing traditionalist tendencies and also with the cultural structures which came into existence in the climate of colonialism, imposing this relationship with the technical and consumerist forms of Western achievement upon us.

The most disturbing aspect of the problem is that the modern Arab poet lives in a state of 'double siege' imposed upon him by the culture of dependency on the one hand, and the culture based on a foetal relationship with the traditionalist past on the other.

What makes this aspect of the problem more serious is the position of the Arabic language itself. The Arab has grown up in a culture which views language as his speaking image, and himself as its feeling, thinking reflection. It is a union of reason and sentiment, the chief symbol and assurance of Arab identity. It is as if language 'created' the Arabs, through instinct in the *Jāhiliyya*, revelation in the prophecy, and reason in Islam; as if originally in the Arab consciousness language was the Supreme Being itself, and its science the science of this Being. From the 'materialness' of this created language the rhythm of existence explodes and its essence pours forth. In this context we can understand the significance of the case endings (*iʿrāb*): they represent the purest principle of language, the sign of unity between the static and the moving, the spoken word and the breath. If language is the rhythmic musical form of nature, then this form only reaches a proper state of wholeness and unity with inflexion.

Language, viewed from this perspective, is not a tool for communicating a detached meaning. It is meaning itself because it is thought. Indeed, it precedes thought and is succeeded by knowledge. This implies that the criterion of meaning was contained in language itself, and was defined by the rules of language.

The problem here is that this language which is regarded in theory as the essence of Arabness appears in practice to be an amorphous heap of words, which some use imperfectly, others abandon in favour of a dialect or foreign tongue and few know how to use creatively. It is like a huge storehouse which people enter, acknowledging their need for it, only to escape from it on some pretext or other. A gap exists between the language and those who speak it. What was once an end is now only a means. How can there be any accommodation between a past which made language the essence of the human being, and a present which sees it only as an instrument and does not hesitate to call for its structure to be modified and for dialects to take its place? If we remember its relation to the sacred, and more precisely to the Qur'ān, can we not see in the current ignorance surrounding its usage or in the call for it to be modified by dialectal structures which separate it from the sacred, a sort of declaration of a changed awareness and identity?

The problematic of modernity at the present time thus becomes clearer at the level of language. What was the first sign of the presence of the Arabs and their creativity is being corrupted and degraded. The Arab of today is in the process of forgetting the fundamental element through which he knew existence, and which established his presence in history. He has lost the sense of language, as defined by Ibn Khaldūn, and appears ignorant of what has given him his identity, or of who he is.

In the light of these considerations it would appear that modernity is the problem of Arab thought in its dialogues with itself and with the history of knowledge in the Arab tradition. If we are to treat the problem of modernity, we must first re-examine the structures of Arab thought. To question modernity, Arab thought must question itself. Arab modernity can be studied only within the perspective of Arab thought, on the level of principles and actual historical developments, within the framework of its specific assumptions, using its epistemological tools and in the context of the issues which gave rise to the phenomenon and have resulted from it. To study it from a Western perspective would be to distort it and distancc oneself from the real issues.

Having acknowledged this, however, we come up against a crisis which, because it has gone on for so long, has become almost a natural phenomenon. I would formulate this crisis as follows: there is a desire in Arab society to separate religion from any form of authority, but there is a contrasting eagerness on the part of the authorities to see religion as one of the foundations of Arab life, its most nearly perfect system, inasmuch as it is divinely revealed, and therefore the key element in guaranteeing the security and stability of the political regime. For this reason politics and religion are bound together in an almost organic relationship.

Thus it is easy to understand why the freedom to ask questions, especially on strictly religious matters, under a regime which relies for its existence on this link, is almost non-existent. In practice politics becomes a sort of submission (*islām*) and an act of faith in the existing regime; anything else is tantamount to rebellion and blasphemy.

This crisis is made more problematic because many of the so-called modern intellectual tendencies striving to separate religion from political power are based on a closed intellectual structure which refuses to accept divine religion but puts another positivist 'religion' in its place.

This crisis constitutes the nucleus around which the dominant structure of thought in Arab society is formed. Both the elements of it which are related to the politico-cultural order and those which characterize the opposition are firmly anchored in the belief that truth is given *a priori* in a text-source which is perfect and definitive. This article of faith, religious or ideological, serves as the all-inclusive founder text; the existing regime, together with its supposed alternative — the opposition which is eager to replace it — is the power which watches over it. Culture is the text which transmits and interprets. Poetry preaches and teaches or instructs and delights. Knowledge is no more than a mirror image of the truths in the all-inclusive founder text.

The flaw is not in the text but in the human being who does not understand it properly or deviates from it. This text contains truth and knowledge. Because it is unique the truth must be unique, because it is its truth, and the same goes for the knowledge. Therefore it is a text which is equated with power. According to this view, truth is always to be found at the heart of power, never outside it. Al-Māwardī (d. 1058), writing in the eleventh century, comments that when a religion loses its authority, its truth is erased. Truth and power form a unity so the division or alteration of power is a division or alteration of truth, which threatens not only truth or power but the Islamic community (*umma*) itself.

This being the case, it is natural that in the eyes of its adherents this text should be absolute, irreplaceable and not open to criticism. The past is defined according to the time when the text came into existence. It is the crucible where all times meet. It is not measured in time, but is itself the measure of time. Decadence lies in distance from this text, failure to adopt it, or deviation from the path traced by it. The *nahḍa* was not an awakening but a return to the past and a firmer attachment to the text. Did not a renaissance in Arab thought, ancient and modern, always represent a return to the prophetic text, the text of the leader and teacher?

This completes the picture of the blockade imposed on us by this crisis: prevailing Arab thought with its two strands, the 'ancient' and the 'modern', is radically opposed to modernity. It is through this crisis-ridden structure of thought that our 'modern' connection with the West and its modernity has been achieved. This has led us to concoct an illusory, specious modernity which is embodied on the practical, day-to-day level in the importation of modern manufactured goods of every kind, and on the level of poetry in plagiarizing forms of expression from languages whose particular genius is intrinsically different from that of Arabic. Thus the intellectual principles which gave birth to modernity are lost to us, their substance wiped out: the unbridled commitment to discovering the mysteries of nature and the unknown aspects of being in deed and word, not for the sake of any return to the past, but to find out more, to proceed, searching and questioning, towards a horizon open to infinity.

The technical, mechanical aspect of modernity is turning our lives into a desert of imported goods and consumption, eating away at us from within and distracting us from thinking about our own distinctive powers of invention. In literature, and in poetry in particular, it generates superficial, naive conceptualizations that interpret modernity simply as a way of arranging and combining words, a mirror held up to everyday life, or an attempt to catch the spray as it flies off the rolling waves of time.

This superficial modernity which is predominant in our societies, engendered partly by a fear of confronting the true state of Arab culture and partly by an understanding which stops at appearances, gives rise to many illusions. I will limit myself to discussing those which act as obstacles to the development of modern poetry.[1]

The first is temporality. There are those who see modernity as the quality of being directly connected with and alive to the present moment. To seize the movement of change in this moment is proof of modernity. It is obvious that these people view time as a series of regular uninterrupted leaps forward, so that what happens today is necessarily an advance on what happened yesterday, and what happens tomorrow is an advance on both. The mistake of this tendency is to turn poetry into a style, ignoring the essential point that the most modern poetry goes beyond the present moment, or goes against it. Poetry does not acquire its modernity merely from being current. Modernity is a characteristic latent in the actual structure of the poetic language.

The second illusion is the desire to be different from the ancient at all costs. Those who adhere to this belief think that merely to be different from what has gone before is proof of modernity. This is an instrumental point of view which turns creativity into a game of opposites, like the doctrine of temporality. One sets 'ancient' time against 'new' time, the other the 'ancient' text against the 'new' text. Thus innovation in poetry resembles waves on the surface of the water, vanishing one after another, despite the fact that a brief glance at the poetry of Abū Nuwās or al-Niffarī, for example, reveals it as more modern than much of the 'counter-poetry' of poets who are alive today.

The third illusion is identification. The West is supposedly the source of modernity. There is no modernity outside Western poetry and its standards: to be modern it is necessary to identify with Western poetry. From this there arises an illusion about norms where standards of modernity in the West, springing from a specific language and experience, become the standards for a language and experience of a different nature. This amounts to looting at a personal, linguistic and poetic level, and is the way to complete alienation.

The fourth illusion is a technical one concerning prose as a poetic form. There are those who believe that simply to write in prose, because it is different from the old metric writing and conforms to models of poetic prose in the West, is a way in to modernity. Some go so far as to say that all metric writing is derivative and old-fashioned and all free verse is innovatory and modernist. This is the reverse of the traditionalist concept that metre in itself is poetry, and prose of whatever kind is the antithesis of poetry. The emphasis is placed not on the substance of poetry but on its external form. Neither metre nor free verse is enough in itself to ensure that the final product will be poetry. We all know verse which has metre and rhyme but is nothing to do with poetry, and supposedly poetic contemporary free verse which is similarly devoid of poetry.

The fifth illusion concerns content. Those who subscribe to this illusion believe that every poetic text which treats contemporary issues is necessarily modern, a claim which does not stand up to examination for a poet can treat these themes according to his intellectual understanding of them, while his artistic approach and manner of expression remain traditional. This is a fault which is all too evident in modern Arabic poetry; from the Iraqis, al-Ruṣāfī (1875–1945) and al-Zahāwī (1863–1936), and the Egyptians, Ḥāfiz Ibrāhīm (1872–1932) and Aḥmad Shawqī, up to the present, there are numerous examples, as there are in the work of all those poets who express their 'modern' ideological beliefs in their poetry.

The poetics of modernity in Arabic was born within a three-stranded movement: there was the urban-sedentary dimension with its own values and symbols (as opposed to the desert and bedouin life), given unique expression and anchored firmly in the literary consciousness by the poetry of Abū Nuwās; the linguistic-metaphoric dimension or the rhetoric of metaphor (as opposed to what may be called 'the rhetoric of reality' of pre-Islamic poetry), expressed for posterity in the poetry of Abū Tammām and the mystic poets; and finally the dimension of interaction and assimilation with non-Arab cultures.

This modernity thus progressed beyond the normative and instead of referring to past authorities began to assert its uniqueness and individuality. It started to innovate, continually renewing the image of things and man's relationship to them, as well as ways of using language and styles of poetic writing. I would stress again that we must place some of the mystics, especially al-Niffarī and Abū Hayyān al-Tawḥīdī (d. 1010), firmly at the heart of this modernist movement, and help rescue them from neglect or oblivion and restore to them the consideration they deserve.[2]

This modernist poetry aroused a storm of criticism amounting in some cases to outright rejection, which was instigated by members of the traditionalist establishment culture and other patrons of the old. The reasons for this criticism can be summarized as follows: the poetry was seen as an attack on the values of the ancient and authentic, and it was this which led to Abū Nuwās being accused of belonging to the Persian-inspired, anti-Arab *Shuᶜūbīyya* movement; it was also seen as an attack on the authentic in poetic expression, held to exist in its exemplary form in ancient poetry, which was why Abū Tammām was said to have 'corrupted Arabic poetry'.[3]

Thus modernity in Arabic poetry had its origins in a climate which brought together two independent elements: awareness of the new urban culture which developed in Baghdad in the eighth century, and a new use of the language to embrace this awareness and express it in poetry. It developed in a spirit of opposition to the ancient, at the same time interacting with non-Arab currents. The whole thrust of Arab civilization testifies to this, for it is a synthesis of the pre-Islamic period and Islam, from whence it derives its origins and heritage, and of other cultures — Persian, Greek and Indian — through adoption and interaction, permeated by the most ancient elements deposited in the historical memory: Sumerian, Babylonian, Aramaean and Syriac.

The effectiveness of Arab creativity at this time demonstrates that no culture exists in isolation from other cultures — they give and take from each other; they influence and are influenced. It also shows that the first condition for this process of interaction is that it should be characterized by creativity and particularity at the same time. This combination carried Arab-Islamic civilization at its most mature to the West by way of Andalusia.

The historical context outlined above demands a re-examination of the course of modernity and the problems it has encountered in its present stage. Such a re-examination must start from an awareness of past events with all their religious, social, political and cultural complexities. This is the only proper way of opening up horizons for understanding the self and the other, allowing us to have a new vision of ourselves and the world, and showing the path we should take in order to build the future. Without this, modernity in Arab society will always be a commodity imported in some underhand way. The society itself will remain a carriage rumbling and swaying along in the wake of the train of Western hegemony, lost between a blind acceptance which robs it of its identity, and an equally blind adherence to the traditionalist past, which robs it of its inventive spirit and prevents it from being a presence in the living reality.

Consciousness of the self forces us to acknowledge that our ancestors' many and varied achievements are not enough in themselves to answer our present problems or lead us to discover a new epistemology. This does not imply a denial of their achievements or their role in the historical process of the production of knowledge. Rather, we should acknowledge that we are confronting issues of which they were unaware; we are therefore bound to approach them in different ways, especially in an age which has witnessed such a tremendous explosion of knowledge. To continue to operate using the old forms of knowledge and within the old boundaries, using the old methods of approach, is to abandon knowledge in its present state, and therefore to abandon knowledge itself.

Continuing in the old ways does not necessarily mean preserving our heritage or holding on to our authenticity. Authenticity is not a fixed point in the past to which we must return in order to establish our identity. It is rather a constant capacity for movement and for going beyond existing limits towards a world which, while assimilating the past and its knowledge, looks ahead to a better future.

What we should take hold of and imitate is the flame of questioning which animated our ancestors, so that we can complement their work with a new vision and new approaches to knowledge. This requires us to dissect their views and intellectual achievements and assimilate them critically so that the new develops out of the old but at the same time is something completely different. This is the only way of ensuring a profound and constructive continuity between the old and the new.

Consciousness of the other assumes a realization on our part that the opposition between the Arab-Islamic East and the

European-American West is not of an intellectual or poetic nature, but is political and ideological, originally a result of Western imperialism. This is why when we reject the West we should not reject it as a whole, but only this ideological aspect of it. Similarly when we reject the automated nature of its technology, this does not mean that we reject technology absolutely or the intellectual principles which led to its invention, but only the way the West uses it and imposes it upon us, in an attempt to buy us and turn us into mere consumers and our countries into market-places. We can learn from the creative energy of the West and its intellectual inventions and construct a dialogue with them, as the West itself did in the past with the products of our civilization. In this way our awareness of the other implies that its achievement is not all devoid of value. There is much in it which we can benefit from, not only in understanding our particular problems, but also in the production of knowledge.

Without such an awareness our political and ideological opposition to the West risks becoming an opposition to its culture and civilization. The desire to consolidate this latter form of opposition, whether it comes from the West or the Arabs, and is deliberate or involuntary, reveals another desire — that of asserting the notion of 'Western superiority', thereby perpetuating the false dualism of the civilized West and the backward East. I say false dualism because it is conceived on the basis of superficial criteria — the criteria of the mechanical and the technical — whereas there no longer exists a 'West' and an 'East', each forming a self-contained conceptual unity. The West contains many 'Wests' more decadent than any Arab decadence, and the Arab East has many 'Easts' more advanced than the most advanced of these Wests.

Seen from this perspective, the world today lives in the climate of a single universal civilization, but one which has its own specificities, obvious or hidden, that depend on the level of creative presence in the various peoples. This suggests that modernity is also a climate of universal forms and ideas and not a state specific to one people. If there is a disparity between the West and the Arab world in the practice of modernity, it is a quantitative disparity of the first order, generated by science in the narrow sense of the word. The level of scientific development is the main characteristic of modernity in the West and the factor which distinguishes it from the East. Modern Western science constitutes a complete epistemological break with the old world, especially with its religious and metaphysical dimensions. It is the area where thought advances unimpeded, more advanced today than yesterday, tomorrow than today. The truths it offers are not like those of philosophy or the arts. They are truths which everyone must of necessity accept, because they are proven in theory and practice.

Science, as a system of knowledge, is constantly self-critical. It moves beyond existing frontiers, does not know words like stasis or retreat, and represents continuous progress because it never ceases to question and search.

The need to transcend the past, or erase it, is therefore self-evident in scientific procedure. The past is error, and authority is sought not from what is past but from what is to come. Western science, with its intuitions and practical results, is the most revolutionary development in the history of mankind.

What does this scientific revolution contain, from a theoretical point of view, of particular relevance for us Arabs? I will try to summarize this in the following four points.

First, science changes human consciousness, engendering in it a new acceptance of astonishing facts which cannot be refuted because of the influence of scientific methodology and the idea that progress is natural and inevitable.

Second, scientific inquiry knows no restrictions or obstacles and refuses to accept any area as inaccessible to it. Scientific research is carried on regardless of the implications for ideas, morals, traditions or other aspects of life.

Third, science completely changes the way in which the past is viewed. In its eyes the past is not only error but also ignorance. Whatever parts of it will not stand up to scientific investigation are rejected as worthless.

Fourth, science makes people open to the idea of a future radically different from anything they have known before, and therefore ready to accept the ending of the past. However hard a person tries to reject science, on either a rhetorical or a technical level, he is doomed to failure. Today scientific invention and discovery are the most important signs of power and superiority. Mechanized industry is spreading to take its place alongside the most deeply rooted traditions and in the most backward societies. Scientific and technical progress are universal realities which cannot be ignored or avoided. They have gradually come to occupy a place in our ideas and awareness, to invade our lives and announce the collapse of the ancient world.

The Arabs have been much influenced by the scientific perspective and the cultural changes brought about by it. To be more precise, I should say that we have been affected in our intellectual awareness and our conscious minds, while our unconscious continues to teem with other things which have escaped the boundaries of scientific rationalism. We continue to come up against this paradox, to which I have already referred: why does Arab society rush to avail itself of the technical achievements of science, and reject its intellectual principles?

Scientific awareness created anxiety and insecurity in us, whereas our unconscious gave us certainty and reassurance. We considered science as a gain at the level of external progress, but a loss in terms of progress in the internal world of intimate human affairs; our consciousness of science therefore thrust us forcefully towards the future, while in our hearts we followed an ill-defined path back to some notion of the past where human warmth was more in evidence.

In this climate (and I will confine myself now to talking only about what happened in modernist poetry) we began to pose our artistic questions in relation to science. For example, what does progress mean in poetry? Nothing. The idea of progress is fundamental to science but quite separate from artistic creativity. Thus we found something which was incompatible with science as progress but was not an irrelevance. We began to deduce that scientific progress was not synonymous with progress as a whole and was therefore not to be used as a norm. Another sort of progress exists on a different level nearer to man and more expressive of the inwardness of his being.

We began to see that the aesthetics of the age we were living in was founded upon and motivated by an idea of resistance to the merely mechanical and technical side of science. This resistance saw a modernity of greater humanity and stature in certain elements of the past. Because the applications of technology were relatively homogeneous, they led to a unformity and sameness which gave life itself a mechanical dimension. Poetry, on the other hand, affirmed difference, giving movement, ebullience and variation to life.

Thus we were split in two, our rational consciousness on the side of science and the future, and our hearts on the side of art and the past. It was as if we were reviving what science had neglected, disregarded or tried to kill off, and this split in us reflected the conflict between freedom and necessity, in this case represented by art and science.

From the perspective of this conflict, I started to see (I speak here only of my own experience and what I say does not necessarily apply to other writers) something inimical to the spirit of poetry in every move to make poetic creation subject to a rationalist scientific precept: one that seemed to say, the future before all else. I began to search for alternative forms which, while not rejecting the notion of the future, did not put an absolute ban on the past. They were forms which, on the contrary, embraced the past in some way: legend, mysticism, magical and non-rational elements of the literary tradition, the mysterious regions of the human soul. I used them to move away from the cold rationalism of science, in my efforts to reveal truths which are more sublime and concern humanity in a more profound way than scientific truths. This return to older sources was not passé, as some commentators described it. It was an attempt to reflect upon and comprehend human existence as a whole, beginning deep down where the reality of this existence was least cluttered by extraneous factors and man lived directly with the land and talked to it in a language which operated at the level of sensation and physical contact, inarticulate cries, instinct and sex. Such a way of proceeding is obviously the opposite of the rational, direct, clear approach, plunging deep into the obscure and terrifying areas which escape the grip of science and rationalism, but where great creation has its beginnings, suspended over the abyss of the undefined and the limitless.

It was therefore a rediscovery, or an attempt to create a starting-point from which to investigate the possibilities for a new direction in human affairs. I saw in legend especially something which afforded me this timeless perspective from which to view the human condition and strengthened my feeling of being one with mankind — a constant present. Through using legends, I was able to witness and journey among the earliest visions conjured up by the human imagination, the earliest motivating forces of behaviour, the first questions and the first inventions.

Thus I began to follow a path which was the opposite both of the scientific path, in the purely technical sense, and of the rationalism on which science is based, or which it gives rise to. Progress began to take on a different meaning in my mind. I gradually became aware that the essence of progress is human, that it is qualitative not quantitative, and that the Westerner who lives surrounded by computers and exposed to the latest in space travel is not necessarily more advanced in any profound sense than the Arab peasant living among trees and cattle.

As a result I came to believe that the progress of a society is not represented merely by economic and social renewal, but more fundamentally by the liberation of man himself, and the liberation of the suppressed elements beneath and beyond the socio-economic structure, in such a way that human beings at their freest and most responsive become both the pivot and the goal.

Technology and rationalism, and, let us say, modernism, have placed human beings within a closed 'mechanical' system. This leads them to focus on their immediate material existence, where all their powers are directed towards dominance in the external world, involving the control and exploitation of the other. It disregards their intimate natures, their passions, needs and desires, and betrays them while declaring that it alone is faithful to them.

The human being is a sublime creature, and there is nothing for him in this modernist technology except the materialism of an attachment to manufactured things, and to quantity. Technology does not cover the whole of existence; it only responds to the needs of an insignificant part of it. Moreover, man is not defined by quantity.

I saw poetry increasingly as the most important means available to humanity of breaking the hold of modern technology and its instrumental rationalism. If technology is the relationship which human beings have established with nature, through scientific rationality, then poetry is the relationship which one human being establishes with the individual essence of another, through nature. When there is no poetry in a period of history, there is no true human dimension. Poetry, according to this definition, is more than a means or a tool, like technology: it is rather, like language itself, an innate quality. It is not a stage in the history of human consciousness but a constituent of this consciousness.

I came to believe that modern technology, with its mechanical, repetitive reliability, had deprived nature of its significance for us and was now robbing the future itself of meaning. The future was no longer that unknown quantity, anticipated with hope and joy, but had begun to appear like a past which we mechanically relived. As a result some forms of the ancient appeared strange and fascinating, compared to the monotonously recurrent forms of modern technology, and the past, especially aspects of it which were officially suppressed or not widely known about, seemed magical and unfamiliar. I felt that we were in deep need of something that went beyond the technological in the direction of those areas which have been more or less obliterated from human memory, and towards the invisible which, however doggedly we try to unveil it and however deeply we penetrate it, remains invisible. Poetry keeps human beings open to the invisible, the hidden, the infinite unknown, always on the threshold of what is to come; at this point, which is both in time and outside time, poetry becomes a bridge joining what a man was, what he is here and now, and what he will be tomorrow in an all-inclusive movement which goes beyond the mechanical, blind indifference of technical progress and embraces the changing unknown.

It appeared to me then that poetic modernity had been incorporated into history, which meant that the concept which I was in the process of discovering became 'ancient'. Perhaps the book which most urgently needs writing today is a history of modernity in Arabic poetry from the eighth century up to the middle of the twentieth.

Modernity as a concept whose fundamental characteristic is opposition to the ancient had ceased to exist. The modern in poetry was not in opposition to the ancient. Gibrān (1883–1931) and al-Sayyāb (1926–64), both 'moderns', share a poetic house with the 'ancients' Imru'l-Qays and Ṭarafa Ibn al-^{c}Abd (538–64), and with Abū Nuwās and Abū Tammām who were 'modern' in relation to the pre-Islamic poets but are today considered 'ancient' when judged in terms of chronological time. All of these poets come together, beyond the simple categories of modern and ancient, in the single melting-pot of poetic creativity, to form what I would call the entirety of authentic Arabic poetry, or, from a historical point of view, 'the second modernity'.

When applied to the poetry of Abū Nuwās and Abū Tammām, modernity meant two things: first, renewal, which was not a rejection of the pre-Islamic tradition, but an affirmation of renewed life; and, second, artistic and intellectual methods of organization in the aesthetic context of this renewal, at the levels of both vision and expression.

The 'modern' in poetry from the beginning of this century up to the publication of the periodical *Shi^{c}r* (Poetry; founded in 1956) was just a maturing and enlarging of perspective, which resulted in the discovery of hitherto unknown dimensions of modernism and led to a re-examination of the definition of poetry itself. The theoretical treatment of this question represented the peak of *Shi^{c}r*'s achievements, in addition to the publication of a body of poetry which set new standards for the way poets approached their subject, and for the understanding and evaluation of poetry. What is advocated in poetry today is merely a continuation of the path established by *Shi^{c}r*.

This continuity of the poetical order confirms that Arab poetic modernity is a part of history and that the modern is also ancient; since nothing radical has been added to it, it cannot be said that the concept of modernity in poetry has altered.

However, just as we witnessed a tyranny of fashion in poetry after Abū Nuwās and Abū Tammām, that is, a tyranny of form, so we are witnessing the same thing today. Although fashion is an attitude which always accompanies modernity, it is at the same time a method and a technique imposed by the world of industry, a world which dominates us and the rest of the globe to an ever greater degree. Young people everywhere are seduced by fashion — it is an expression of their desire to assert that they have broken away from their parents, or from the past as represented by the stable traditional establishment which appears to them, from the undisciplined turbulence of modern life, to be stagnant and unresponsive to their aspirations.

The overriding characteristic of fashion is its artificiality; by this I mean that, like anything artificial, it is transient and ephemeral. Second, fashion cancels out what has gone before: today's fashion is superior to yesterday's. To embrace the natural involves going outside the self in order to penetrate the self more deeply and be restored to a wholeness; to espouse the artificiality of passing styles, on the other hand, means deserting the self to be tossed here and there like a leaf in the wind. The first way takes in all ages and all times, but the second delights in gliding over the surface of the moment. So the artificial, in the shape of a whimsical notion about artistic form, seems to become part of the past at its inception, and fashion for fashion's sake is outmoded or 'ancient' in advance.

Therefore it became clear to me that modernity was both of time and outside time: of time because it is rooted in the movement of history, in the creativity of humanity, coexisting with man's striving to go beyond the limitations which surround him; and outside time because it is a vision which includes in it all times and cannot only be recorded as a chronological event: it cuts vertically through time and its horizontal progress is no more than the surface representation of a deep internal movement. In other words, modernity is not only a process that affects language; it is synonymous with its very existence. Modernity in poetry in any language is first of all modernity of the language itself. Before you can be a 'modern' or an 'ancient' in poetry you have to be a poet, and you cannot be a poet until you feel or write as if you are your language and it is you. As language is a vocal, musical and social value, it has a history and a past. Without a knowledge of this past, modernity is not possible. Moreover, the language of modernity can have no value independent of the history of the creative genius of the language. In any language, the establishing of a new artistic value relies first of all on a comprehensive understanding and assimilation of whatever is of value in the history of that language.

The artistic difference or divergence to which modernist poetic writing gives authority can only be defined within the artistic context of a given language, and the conflict which occurs at this point is only in fact a process of accommodation. The old and the new in poetry are two faces of a single creativity. The new in Arabic poetry, for example, however unequivocal its formal break with the past may appear, is nevertheless identifiably Arab in character; by this I mean that it cannot be understood or evaluated within the context of French or English modernism, or according to their criteria, but must be seen in the context of Arab creativity and judged by the standards of artistic innovation particular to Arabic.

I will conclude with some observations which provide a framework to our understanding of the particular nature of poetics and modernity in Arabic. First, I want to stress that modernity requires not only freedom of thought, but physical freedom as well. It is an explosion, a liberation of what has been suppressed. To think and write what is truly new means above all to think about what has never been thought about and write what has never been written: that huge, constant area of suppression — religious and cultural, individual and social, spiritual and physical. This implies that modernity is an immersion in history, a kind of writing which subjects this history to constant questioning, and a form of self-awareness that exposes writing itself to constant scrutiny within the framework of a continuous exercise to discover the powers of language and investigate the possibilities and limitations of experiment. The Arabic language and Arab society are not two primitive plants but have firm roots reaching deep into history; it is these roots which provide the context for and the means of achieving modernity. Thus a knowledge of the origins of their 'ancient' forms, the changes they underwent and the problems they encountered, especially with regard to the mysteries of the particular genius of the language, is essential to an understanding of the 'modern'. For an Arab poet to be truly modern his writing must glow like a flame which rises from the fire of the ancient, but at the same time is entirely new.

If Arab poetic modernity is partly based on the liberation of what has been suppressed — that is, on the expression of desire — and on everything that undermines the existing repressive norms and values, and transcends them, then ideological concepts like 'authenticity', 'roots', 'heritage', 'renaissance' and 'identity' take on different meanings. Traditional notions of the continuous, the coherent, the one, the complete, are replaced by the interrupted, the confused, the plural, the incomplete, implying that the relationship between words and things is constantly changing: that is, there is always a gap between them which saying or writing the words cannot fill. This unbridgeable gap means that the questions 'What is knowledge?', 'What is truth?', 'What is poetry?' remain open, that knowledge is never complete and that truth is a continuing search.

The essence of this is that modernity should be a creative vision, or it will be no more than a fashion. Fashion grows old from the moment it is born, while creativity is ageless. Therefore not all modernity is creativity but creativity is eternally modern.

Notes

Chapter 1

1. Al-Marzubānī, *al-Muwashshaḥ*, p. 39.

2. Ibn Rashīq, *al-*^{c}*Umda fī Mahāsin al-Shi*^{c}*r wa Adabihi wa Naqdihi* (Cairo, 1934), vol. I, p. 15.

3. Ibid., p. 9.

4. Ibn Khaldūn, *al-Muqaddima* (Beirut, 1967).

5. Ibid., p. 488.

6. For more details about poetry and the recitation of poetry, see ^{c}Alī al-Jundī, *al-Shu*^{c}*arā' wa Inshād al-Shi*^{c}*r* (Dār al-Ma^{c}ārif, Cairo, 1969).

7. See *Lisān al-*^{c}*Arab*: *saj*^{c}.

8. Ibn Khaldūn, *al-Muqaddima*, p. 569.

9. Al-Jāḥiẓ, *Kitāb al-Bayān wa'l-Tabyīn* (Cairo 1960), vol. II, p. 7.

10. Ṭaha Ḥusayn, *Ḥadīth al-Shi*^{c}*r wa'l-Nathr*, 2nd edn (Cairo), p. 90.

11. Ibn Khaldūn, *al-Muqaddima*, p. 454.

12. Ibid., p. 455.

13. It is said that al-Khalīl discussed many subjects: song and rhythm, theology and dialectics, chess and backgammon among others. 'He had a knowledge of melody and the distribution of sounds which led him to become a pioneer in the study of prosody . . . He also wrote a book about song and rhythm and

called it *Tarākīb al-Aṣwāt* (The Structures of Sounds).' For this and further information, see Mahdī al-Makhzūmī's important study of al-Khalīl.

14. Al-Fārābī, *Kitāb al-Mūsīqā al-Kabīr*, p. 1,181.
15. Ibid., p. 436.
16. Ibid., p. 1,088.
17. Al-Jurjānī, *Dalā'il al-I^{c}jāz* (Cairo, 1969), p. 485.
18. Ibn Ṭabāṭabā, *^{c}Iyār al-Shi^{c}r* (Cairo, 1956), p. 119.
19. Ibid., p. 128.
20. Al-Āmidī, *al-Muwāzana*, vol. I, p. 191.
21. Al-Jāḥiẓ, *Kitāb al-Bayān wa'l-Tabyīn*, vol. I, p. 118.
22. See Abū Hayyān al-Tawhīdī, *al-Imtā^{c} wa'l-Mu'ānasa* (Beirut), vol. II, pp. 140–3.
23. Al-Fārābī, *Kitāb al-Mūsīqā al-Kabīr*, p. 1,093.
24. Al-Jāḥiẓ, *Kitāb al-Bayān wa'l-Tabyīn*, vol. I, p. 82.
25. Ibid., vol. III, p. 26.
26. Ibid., vol. III, pp. 24–5.
27. Ibid., vol. I, p. 79.

Chapter 2

1. Here, briefly, are some of the major titles: Abū ^{c}Ubayda, *Naqā'iḍ Jarīr wa'l-Farazdaq* (The Polemics of Jarīr and al-Farazdaq); al-Qurashī (eighth century), *Jamharat Ash^{c}ār al-^{c}Arab* (Anthology of the Poems of the Arabs); al-Ashnāndānī (eighth century), *Ma^{c}ānī al-Shi^{c}r* (The Meanings of Poetry); Qudāma Ibn Ja^{c}far (d. 958), *Naqd al-Nathr* (A Critique of Prose); Abū Hilāl al-^{c}Askarī (d. 1005), *Kitāb al-Ṣinā^{c}atayn, al-Shi^{c}r wa'l-Nathr* (The Book of the Two Arts: Poetry and Prose).
2. Quoted in al-Baghdādi, *al-Farq bayna al-Firaq* (The Difference Between the Schisms) in a chapter entitled 'The Fifteenth Scandal'.
3. Al-Jurjānī, *Dalā'il al-I^{c}jāz* (Cairo, 1969), 'Introduction'.
4. Ibid., pp. 40–1.

5. Ibid., p. 38.
6. Ibid., p. 70.
7. Ibid., pp. 196–7.
8. Ibid., pp. 51, 67.
9. Ibid., p. 20.
10. Ibid., p. 364.
11. Al-Jurjānī, *Asrār al-Balāgha* (Cairo, 1959), p. 26.
12. Ibid., pp. 40–1.
13. Ibid., pp. 116, 118.
14. Ibid., p. 144.
15. Ibid., p. 151.
16. Ibid., pp. 132, 140.
17. Ibid., p. 188.
18. Ibid., p. 128.
19. Ibid., pp. 60, 80–1, 84.
20. Ibid., p. 144.
21. Ibid., p. 138.
22. Ibid., p. 159.
23. Al-Jurjānī, *Dalā'il al-I^{c}jāz*, p. 255.
24. Al-Jurjānī, *Asrār al-Balāgha*, pp. 317–18.

Chapter 3

1. The same can be said of much of the poetry of al-Shanfara (seventh century), ^{c}Urwa Ibn al-Ward (d. 596), al-Samaw'al (d. 560), al-Afwa al-Awdī (d. 570), ^{c}Alqama al-Faḥl (d. 598), Zuhayr Ibn Abī Sulmā (530–627), Ṭarafa Ibn al-^{c}Abd (538–64), ^{c}Adiy Ibn Zayd (d. 587), Labīd Ibn Rabī^{c}a (560–661) and ^{c}Abīd Ibn al-Abraṣ (d. 554).
2. See *Lisān al-^{c}Arab*: *sha^{c}ara*.
3. Ibn Jinnī, *al-Khaṣā'iṣ*, vol. II, pp. 442–7.

Chapter 4

1. For further discussion of these illusions see Adonis, *Fātiḥa*

li-Nihāyāt al-Qarn (Beirut, 1980).

2. Space does not permit an analysis of the characteristics of this aspect of modernity. Those who wish to have a better understanding of my own particular view may refer to the following: *al-Thābit wa'l-Mutaḥawwil, Ta'ṣīl al-Uṣūl*, 3rd edn (Beirut 1982); *Ṣadmat al-Ḥadātha*, 3rd edn (Beirut, 1982); *Fātiḥa li-Nihāyāt al-Qarn; Muqaddima li'l-Shi*ᶜ*r al-*ᶜ*Arabī*, 3rd edn (Beirut, 1979).

3. What needs to be examined is the fact that the same two 'charges' are being levelled at modernity in Arabic poetry today, but with far greater ferocity.

Index of Names